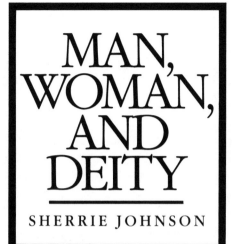

MAN, WOMAN, AND DEITY

SHERRIE JOHNSON

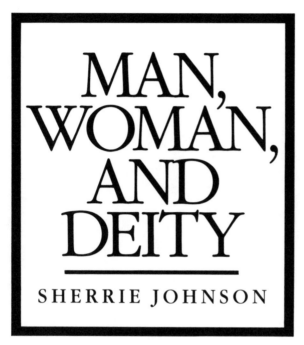

MAN, WOMAN, AND DEITY

SHERRIE JOHNSON

BOOKCRAFT
Salt Lake City, Utah

Library of Congress Catalog Card Number: 91-70219

ISBN 0-88494-788-2

First Printing, 1991

Printed in the United States of America

To the best part of me
Carl Matthew Johnson

And the Lord God said, It is not good that the man should be alone; I will make him an help meet for him.

—Genesis 2:18

Contents

Acknowledgments

A book like this is never really the work of one person. I owe much to teachers who have planted ideas and given me direction. I also owe much to friends who have discussed ideas, shared knowledge, critiqued rough drafts, and most of all encouraged me along the way.

To Sharon Larsen, Ivan Cornia, Christena Nelson, Richard Lemon, Cathy Bubert, Roger Peterson, Diane Hunt, Gerald Lund, Daniel H. Ludlow, Wendy Hill, Dr. Randy Reese, Craig and Renon Hulet, Char Mills, Dr. S. Ray Sumsion, Karen Bell, Kaye Smith and Laurie Thornton I give my thanks and love for help given. And to the staff at Bookcraft, especially George Bickerstaff and Cory Maxwell, a very special thank you for making it all possible and for being so delightful to work with.

But even more, I owe a great thank you to my husband, Carl, and to my children, Boyd and Laresa Campbell, Jay Dee and Talena Kerr, David and Breana Tilley, Anissa, Mariah, Kirsha, Meleah, Patrea, and Joshua for putting up with a mother and wife who is often "in another world" trying to figure things out.

*Through wisdom is an house builded; and by understand-
ing it is established: and by knowledge shall the chambers
be filled with all precious and pleasant riches.*
—Proverbs 24:3-4

CHAPTER 1

Why Differing
Stewardships?

We had only been married three and a half years when my husband,
Carl, and I encountered one of my former high school teachers. An
excellent teacher, she had encouraged me both inside and outside
of the classroom, so I was excited to see her. We chatted for a while
and she asked me what I was now doing. I told her that I had two
young children and they kept me busy. I didn't need to tell her that
the third child was on the way. Her lips tightened as she looked up
and then down my swollen body and said, "I hope you haven't
abandoned the use of your good mind and talents!"

How Will We Teach Our Children?

At the time, I didn't pay much attention to her remark. I was
aware of her outspoken views on LDS marriages and women's
issues and was comfortable with my own views. It wasn't until later
as my daughters and their friends, both male and female, were in
our home and talked of things they were being taught in school

that I became concerned. Part of my comfort with the "traditional" role of women came from my experience with marriage and mothering; I had a personal conviction of the value of this role. These young people did not have that experience to weigh against the things they were being taught—things which often sounded very logical and enticing. I began to see that I was comfortable in believing my former teacher's views were wrong, but that I didn't know enough about what was right to teach truth in place of fallacy. I was suddenly aware that knowing something is wrong is not enough; you can only fight error with truth. So I began to study.

Understanding Stewardships Enriches Marriage

It was only as I began to search for answers to the question, "What is the Lord's purpose for male and female?" that I began to see a second reason why better understanding was vital. The husband and wife relationship is *the* most important relationship any two mortals ever establish. It is a relationship necessary for exaltation. Yet in my stage of "comfortable" I had kept myself from learning about what God intended that relationship to be.

Those who understand the gospel know that even though they have been married in the temple, for that marriage to truly be eternal it must be sealed by the Holy Spirit of Promise. For this reason and many others, some of the best-attended classes, firesides, or conferences deal with making better marriages. Almost every couple wants a smoother, happier marriage. But too often we seek gimmicks and "to-do lists" without really understanding what we are building. It's like trying to build a house without ever having seen a house or even a house plan. We might have marvelous resources of lumber, nails, bricks, wire, sheetrock, paint, and light fixtures, but if we have no concept of what one can build with these materials they don't become rooms or give off any light.

And there is more. A correct understanding of male and female stewardships and the purpose of marriage enhances not only the marriage but all of life. In 1839 the Prophet Joseph Smith taught Parley P. Pratt about celestial marriage. Afterward Brother Pratt recorded the following:

> I had loved before, but I knew not why. But now I loved—with a pureness—an intensity of elevated, exalted feeling, which would

lift my soul from the transitory things of this grovelling sphere and expand it as the ocean. I felt that God was heavenly Father indeed; that Jesus was my brother, and that the wife of my bosom was an immortal, eternal companion; a kind of ministering angel, given to me as a comfort, and a crown of glory for ever and ever. In short, I could now love with the spirit and with the understanding also. (*Autobiography of Parley P. Pratt* [Salt Lake City: Deseret Book Company, 1976], p. 298.)

As I began to search and find answers—to see the "house" —my amazement at the magnificence of the plan of salvation was renewed. I was amazed to find (though I shouldn't have been!) that the plan of salvation is dependent upon the roles of male and female. The more I learned, the clearer my picture became of what I was working toward in my own marriage, and I came to realize that many of my own struggles in marriage had been caused by my lack of understanding. These same kinds of misunderstanding are responsible for many divorces and are often the cause of unhappiness within marriage. You can do everything on the "Do for a Good Marriage" lists and still have problems if you do not understand what the Lord intended marriage to be.

One of the most important teachings of the gospel is that marriage is ordained of God and is a requirement for exaltation. Elder Bruce R. McConkie explained the centrality of the marriage covenant: "Everything that we do in the Church is connected and associated with and tied into the eternal order of matrimony that God has ordained. Everything that we do from the time that we become accountable through all our experiences, and all the counsel and direction we receive up to the time of marriage, is designed and intended to prepare us to enter into a probationary marriage arrangement, one that does in fact become eternal if we abide in the covenant made in connection with that order of matrimony." (*1977 Devotional Speeches of the Year, BYU Devotional and Twelve-Stake Fireside Addresses* [Provo, Utah: Brigham Young University Press, 1978], p. 171.)

Good marriages, the kind that will be eternal and are necessary to lead one to godhood, can be achieved *only* by a correct understanding of maleness and femaleness. Is it any wonder that Satan has caused so much misunderstanding over these principles? Hundreds of years of apostasy and the changing of precepts to fit the philosophies of men have clouded our vision and introduced into our culture traditions that keep us from establishing good relationships.

As Latter-day Saints striving for celestial marriages, we need to discover what part the Lord intended men and women to play in the great plan of salvation. We need to know how males and females should work together to complement and balance each other in order to make the great plan work in their lives. Most important, we need to understand that God has great love for both his sons and his daughters. If we don't come to know what the Lord intends, it will be easy for Satan to make the philosophies of the world begin to sound logical and right not only to our children but also to us.

During the last few years more Latter-day Saint men and women have begun to wonder exactly what the relationship between male and female should be. They sense that what has been handed to them by culture and tradition is not always correct and that a better understanding of these things would enrich their lives, their families, and especially their marriages. They are discovering that the equality of men and women is an integral part of the gospel. Unlike the world, however, which claims that equality is found in sameness, the gospel teaches us that equality is found in balance. As President Joseph Fielding Smith explained:

> There is nothing in the teachings of the gospel which declares that men are superior to women. The Lord has given unto men the power of the priesthood and sent them forth to labor in his service. A woman's calling is in a different direction. The most noble, exalting calling of all is that which has been given to women as the mothers of men. Women do not hold the priesthood, but if they are faithful and true, they will become priestesses and queens in the kingdom of God, and that implies that they will be given authority. (*Doctrines of Salvation*, comp. Bruce R. McConkie, 3 vols. [Salt Lake City: Bookcraft, 1954-56], 3:178.)

In addition, Elder Bruce R. McConkie explained: "Where spiritual things are concerned, as pertaining to all of the gifts of the Spirit, with reference to the receipt of revelation, the gaining of testimonies, and the seeing of visions, in all matters that pertain to godliness and holiness and which are brought to pass as a result of personal righteousness—in all these things men and women stand in a position of absolute equality before the Lord" ("Our Sisters from the Beginning," *Ensign*, January 1979, p. 61).

The gospel of Jesus Christ offers women and men more than can be found *anywhere* else. The blessings, the progression, the peace, and the joy are far beyond anything the world can offer. But to partake of this joy and peace we must understand our interdependency as male and female in terms of our eternal destiny and then build marriages based upon that understanding.

Considering the eternal significance of marriage and the everlasting consequences of how well we perform our duties, is it any surprise that the Bible begins by establishing symbolically and specifically the relationship between man and woman? The very position of the teaching in scripture indicates that the subjects of maleness and femaleness are basic to the gospel of Jesus Christ. In order for us to grow, to progress in the gospel, and to have the happiness we desire in our marriages, we must understand the proper relationship between men and women.

At a BYU Education Week, Brother Chauncey Riddle said (as recorded in my notes): "Right now the Church is known for its large families. It will become a light to the world, however, only when it becomes known for its good marriages." Good marriages can happen only as *both* men and women discover for themselves what the Lord intended when he created man and the help meet, woman.

Fulfilling Our Destinies

Another reason to learn of male and female is so that we can quit relying on hearsay or tradition for our definitions of the male and female roles. Each of us must accept the responsibility of learning what the Lord intends for us so that we can do it. President Brigham Young once counseled: "Were your faith concentrated upon the proper object, your confidence unshaken, your lives pure and holy, every one fulfilling the duties of his or her calling according to the Priesthood and capacity bestowed upon you, you would be filled with the Holy Ghost, and it would be as impossible for any man to deceive and lead you to destruction as for a feather to remain unconsumed in the midst of intense heat" (*Journal of Discourses* 7:277).

The reasons for studying the male-female relationship, then, are many and significant. We each must learn so that we can (1) teach correct concepts to our children and others we influence, (2) make our marriages richer and happier, and (3) fulfill our own destinies.

In the following chapters we will examine the scriptures to see how God set up the male-female relationship. We will examine more closely what is said in the scriptures about the female role than what is said about the male role, because that is the subject on which most of the misunderstanding exists. With that foundation, we will then examine the concepts of priesthood and help meet and discuss the relationship of these complementary stewardships in marriage in order to give us a blueprint of what kind of "building" a marriage should be.

The scriptures are rich with the information we need. The story of Adam and Eve gives us the marriage model and shows us how it was established. Learning from their relationship prior to the Fall helps us to know what the Lord considers an eternal union to be and what we need to do to have a celestial marriage. When we examine what happened to that relationship after the Fall, we gain a great deal of perspective as to what we need to beware of. Comparing the before and the after with our own relationships as husbands and wives gives us a guide as to how we should and should not interact. So let us begin "in the beginning."

And again, verily I say unto you, that whoso forbiddeth to marry is not ordained of God, for marriage is ordained of God unto man.

—D&C 49:15

CHAPTER 2

In the Beginning

Why does the Bible start with the creation of the world and not with the account of the Council in Heaven, as chronology would suggest? Why has the Lord added in our day the books of Moses and Abraham and other sacred teachings that retell the story of the Creation? Why so many narratives of the same story? Taking into account that repetition is the greatest teacher, perhaps the best question is, What is it the Lord is so anxious for us to learn from these accounts?

The creation story is one of a home (earth) being made. A father (our Heavenly Father) supervises the creation of the home, while Jesus Christ and others carry out the details. Even though it was to be a home for mortals, mortals could not have created it alone. As we go about creating our homes, it is wise to remember that very important principle.

After everything was carefully prepared, a man was placed upon the earth to take care of it—the same man who helped in its creation (just as each of us must also live with what we have created). Adam's life in the garden was very different from what we know now or from what he had known in his premortal existence. Elder Bruce R. McConkie reminded us: "Adam was still in the presence of God, with whom he walked and talked and from whom he received counsel and commandments. (Moses 3:4.) He had temporal life because his spirit was housed in a temporal body, one made from the dust of the earth. (Abraham 5:7.) He had spiritual life because he was in the presence of God and was alive to the things of righteousness or of the Spirit." (*Mormon Doctrine,* 2nd ed. [Salt Lake City: Bookcraft, 1966], p. 268.)

Because Adam was alive to the things of the Spirit he was one with God. But he did not comprehend or have knowledge of good and evil. He did not know whether he was happy or sad or whether he loved or hated. He did not know whether what he was experiencing was good or evil. But even more, he did not know that happy or sad or good or evil even existed. Having no way of experiencing suffering or pain, joy or pleasure, sorrow or happiness, he could not make choices which would allow him to progress.

The scriptures record some of the instructions God gave Adam concerning this new home. The course of life and existence, not only for Adam but for all mankind, was dependent upon these instructions. As mortal parents we often struggle with what advice will be best when sending a child away to school or on a mission or to be married. What information did an omniscient God give to man that would best help him achieve his full potential and purpose as he began mortality? God told Adam about the tree of knowledge of good and evil and the tree of life. He carefully explained the situation; the choices that were available to Adam, and the consequences that would occur for each choice. Then God declared: "It is not good that the man should be alone: I will make him an help meet for him" (Genesis 2:18).

One would expect the next verse to be about the creation of the help meet, but it isn't. Instead God reinforces this second declaration with the first object lesson in recorded history. Adam is given an assignment to name all the animals as they come to him. None of the accounts tells us how long this took, but it sounds like a rather time-consuming job. Perhaps for weeks or months or even more the male and female animals paraded before Adam, and he named them.

In many languages there is both a feminine and masculine form for nouns. For example, in the Hebrew, from which our Old

Testament came, a male horse is *soos* and a female horse or mare *soosa*. We don't know what Adam named the animals or whether he used gender in naming them, but it is interesting to ponder what he might have thought as the animals came before him and he saw that every other creature came in both a male and a female version. Did he feel lonely as he saw male and female of every species? But "as for Adam," we are told, "there was not found an help meet for him" (Moses 3:20; Genesis 2:20). Apparently this was soon remedied (see Abraham 5:21).

A Help Meet for Man

It seems that only after Adam had seen and named all the animals and recognized his own incompleteness in comparison did the Lord provide the promised help meet. Finally "the Lord God caused a deep sleep to fall upon Adam, and he slept: and he took one of his ribs, and closed up the flesh instead thereof; and the rib, which the Lord God had taken from man, made he a woman, and brought her unto the man" (Genesis 2:21–22).

Adam responded, "This I know now is bone of my bones, and flesh of my flesh; she shall be called Woman, because she was taken out of man" (Moses 3:23; see also Genesis 2:23). Because of his experience with the animals, Adam recognized this help meet as his true counterpart. It would be interesting to know the exact word Adam used for woman. While our English words *man* and *woman* show some relationship, the original word probably more meaningfully expressed the concept of woman being taken out of man.

We must be careful that the words *help meet* that are used to describe the woman are not confused with the word *helpmate*. Modern usage has made the two words, *help meet*, into one word, but that obscures the meaning. The original Hebrew word in this scripture is *ezer*, which was translated "help" in the Genesis account. Too often we think of the word *help* as meaning assistant or servant, but that connotation suggests a subordinate position, whereas man and woman are equal. So what does *help* mean in this case? Another definition of the word *help* is "to remedy, alleviate, cure." This fits the meaning of *ezer*, for in other places in the Old Testament *ezer* is used to describe Deity. As a matter of fact, of the twenty-one occurrences of the word *ezer* in the Old Testament record, sixteen refer to God. "Behold, God is mine helper" (Psalm 54:4) and "Lord, be thou my helper" (Psalm 30:10) are examples of this usage. Certainly God is not our helper in the sense of being a subordinate assistant or servant, but God is our remedy, our cure, our help in that he atoned for our sins and alleviated the problems caused by the Fall. The adjective *meet* means suitable, proper, or appropriate. Thus a help meet is a suitable remedy, an appropriate cure or appropriate help.

But for what was the woman an appropriate cure? Woman remedied man's incompleteness. She was literally his cure, his restoration to a healthy condition. Alone he was limited, he needed help to be completed in the image of God; he could not have children and he could not fully use his priesthood because there was no one to use it on. Thus he was deficient without the woman. Her creation and subsequent union with him, then, was a remedy or cure that alleviated his incompleteness. Together man and woman were to "multiply, and replenish the earth, and subdue it: and have dominion over the fish of the sea, and over the fowl of the air, and over every living thing that moveth upon earth" (Genesis 1:28). The man could not do that alone. Elder Joseph Fielding Smith explained that the woman was "a help who would answer all the requirements, not only of companionship, but also through whom the fulness of the purposes of the Lord could be accomplished regarding the mission of man through mortal life and into eternity" (*Doctrines of Salvation*, comp. Bruce R. McConkie, 3 vols. [Salt Lake City: Bookcraft, 1954–56], 2:70).

Man to Cleave to His Wife

In all three narratives, Genesis, Moses, and Abraham, we next find: "Therefore shall a man leave his father and his mother, and shall cleave unto his wife; and they shall be one flesh" (Moses 3:24). *Therefore* means "for that reason" or "because" and refers back to verse 23, which tells of the creation of woman. Because woman was taken out of man and is bone of Adam's bones and flesh of Adam's flesh, when returned to him she is a remedy for his incompleteness, a help meet. Therefore a man shall leave his father and his mother and shall cleave unto a wife; and they shall be everlastingly whole and complete.

Of all the different words that Joseph Smith might have used in this verse, to convey the meaning of the revelation he received, such as "stay with" or "cling to," he chose to keep the same word as the King James Bible: *cleave.* In English there are two definitions for the word *cleave:* (1) To part or divide along natural lines of separation and (2) to stick fast; adhere, to be faithful to. The same word —strangely!—means both to sever and to unite; just as the woman was first severed from the man, but in marriage the two are united.

After quoting from Genesis 2:24, Elder LeGrand Richards wrote:

> It is evident that the Lord did not have in mind that they should be one in purpose and desire, for he makes himself clear as to what this oneness should consist of: "one flesh."
>
> Jesus understood this principle fully, as we learn from his statement: "For this cause shall man leave his father and mother, and cleave to his wife; And they twain shall be one flesh: so then they are no more twain, but one flesh. What therefore God hath joined together, let no man put asunder." (Mark 10:7-9.)
>
> Thus Jesus gave us to understand that both man and wife should be "one flesh." ("The Eternal Companionship: Husband and Wife," in *Woman* [Salt Lake City: Deseret Book Company, 1979], p. 41.)

When God made Eve Adam's wife, commanding them to be one flesh, time did not exist on earth, hence their union was to be forever. Thus the word *cleave* takes on the added significance of being a bond that was meant to endure eternally.

Adam was already one with God, and now he was to be one with the woman also. In this way was formed a triangular relationship of God, man, and woman, with God advising and directing the partnership. This is the perfect "Eden" relationship.

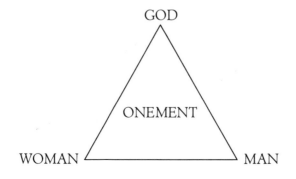

Made from a Rib

It is also interesting to consider the symbolism employed by the figurative use of Adam's rib as the material from which the woman was formed. Symbolically Adam was made from dust of the earth, but the woman was made from bone. They were made of different materials and for different purposes. It seems she was not made of Adam's muscle to move him or be moved by him. She was not taken from his heart so she would feel as he felt, or from his mind so that she would think as he thought. Instead the woman was made of Adam's bone, the part of the body that gives structure and stature and where the marrow which produces the life-giving element of mortality—blood—is found.

With a rib removed (figuratively), a piece of Adam was missing. He was incomplete. In order to be whole again he had to replace or "cleave unto" the missing part. As he married and became one flesh with the woman, he took back the missing piece. The Hebrew word for bride, *kallah*, illustrates this concept. *Kallah* is derived from the primary root *kalal*, which means to complete or to make perfect. This completion that came when a man married added stature and structure and marrow to the man. He was whole once more, and the woman, symbolically a rib, also was returned to completeness. Alone both the man and the woman remain incomplete, unfinished, lacking a part.

This symbolism of oneness or "onement" is intensified when we learn that in the scriptures the man and the woman shared the same name until after the Fall. "Male and female created he them; and blessed them, and *called their name Adam*, in the day when they were created" (Genesis 5:2; Moses 6:9, italics added).

Fall and Separation

In the Moses account (Moses 4:1-6), some verses of instruction interjected at this point in the story almost seem out of context until we analyze them a little more closely. These verses take us back to the account of our premortal life and explain that Satan, before the world was created, volunteered to redeem all mankind— and also to receive all honor and glory and power for doing so. But this was a rebellion against the Father's plan. Satan was rejected in favor of another son of God, Jesus Christ, who offered to fulfill the Father's plan. Because of this rejection, Satan started a war among the spirit children of the Father and was consequently cast out of the presence of the Father and sent to earth with those who followed him, never to have the chance to receive a mortal body or be united with a counterpart.

This piece of instruction to Moses, placed here in the account, is significant in helping us understand Satan's motivations for what follows. Adam and Eve now begin their work on the earth and Satan tries to thwart them. (Identifying what Satan wants to destroy is a reliable way of defining the most important things in life.) Satan's wicked efforts are aimed at separating Adam and Eve. He does not want them to be united, to be true counterparts, to be completed in the image of God, to be as God is. He wants them to be alone, separate, incomplete, as he is. Therefore, Satan approaches Eve when she is not with Adam and tempts her to eat of the forbidden fruit. He tells a series of half truths and succeeds in enticing Eve to partake. This was a serious mistake for two reasons: 1) the fruit was forbidden and 2) Eve failed to consult with Adam, her counterpart, concerning the decision. Two people cannot be one if they do not share in all the decisions that concern the partnership.

This was a victory for Satan. The man and the woman were now very different. Eve was no longer innocent. They were no longer one. They could not even remain in the same place, but would be physically separated. But Satan was not satisfied. The triangle was broken, but Adam was still innocent. Satan must also separate God and Adam so that no piece of the triangle remained.

The woman then did what she should have done before—she consulted with her husband, and we might say that the first recorded "executive session of family council" was held. The fact that after their discussion Adam himself chose to partake makes a very firm statement concerning the importance of "onement." Adam could have said: "I don't want to have anything more to do with her. She has rebelled against God." He could have justified himself in many ways; he was still innocent, she was not. But he chose not to do that. He reasoned through the alternatives before him, recognized how important it was that they remain together and partake of mortality, and ate the fruit. This was a decision neither of them regretted, despite the drastic changes it made in their lives. Adam later testified: "Blessed be the name of God, for because of my transgression my eyes are opened, and in this life I shall have joy, and again in the flesh I shall see God. And Eve, his wife, heard all these things and was glad, saying: Were it not for our transgression we never should have had seed, and never should have known good and evil, and the joy of our redemption, and the eternal life which God giveth unto all the obedient. And Adam and Eve blessed the name of God, and they made all things known unto their sons and their daughters." (Moses 5:10–12.)

But all was not as perfect as it was before. Satan once more set to work, this time trying to prevent the reestablishment of the relationship triangle. His goal is to come between the man and the woman and God in any way he can. He delights in dwelling upon and driving wedges into "natural lines of separation" such as the line between man and woman or between mortal and God.

The first thing that happened was that the man and the woman became ashamed of their nakedness; this shame was a symbol of their sin and consequent vulnerability. No longer being one with God, they tried to hide from him. On other occasions they had conversed with God and looked forward to his coming; but this time they were afraid.

There is a difference between the Moses account and the Genesis account at this point. God returns to the garden. In the Genesis account he asks, "Where art thou?" In the Moses account, the question is much more poignant: "Where goest thou?"

The second rendering helps us understand the Lord's intentions in asking. An all-knowing God already knew Adam's physical location. The question instead seems to be concerned with the soul's direction and was meant to teach Adam and each of us. It carries the implication, Do you understand where your choices are taking you? Adam answered, however, according to location.

> And he said: I heard thy voice in the garden, and I was afraid, because I beheld that I was naked, and I hid myself.
> And I, the Lord God, said unto Adam: Who told thee thou wast naked? Hast thou eaten of the tree whereof I commanded thee that thou shouldst not eat, if so thou shouldst surely die?
> And the man said: The woman thou gavest me, and commandest that she should remain with me, she gave me of the fruit of the tree and I did eat.

And I, the Lord God, said unto the woman: What is this thing which thou hast done? And the woman said: The serpent beguiled me, and I did eat. (Moses 4:16–19.)

Consequences for Mortality

Consequences now became apparent. Satan had more tools with which to separate the man and the woman from each other and from God. But God revealed more helps for uniting them. The great plan of salvation moved forward. Enmity was placed between the seed of the woman and Satan. Elder James E. Talmage explained this by saying:

> Brief mention of the plan of salvation, the author of which is Jesus Christ, appears in the promise given of God following the fall— that though the devil, represented by the serpent in Eden, should have power to bruise the heel of Adam's posterity, through the seed of the woman should come the power to bruise the adversary's head. It is significant that this assurance of eventual victory over sin and its inevitable effect, death, both of which were introduced to earth through Satan the arch-enemy of mankind, was to be realized through the offspring of woman; the promise was not made specifically to the man, nor to the pair.

Elder Talmage also said, "In our Lord alone has been fulfilled the word of God spoken in relation to the fall of Adam, that the *seed of the woman* should have power to overcome Satan by bruising the serpent's head." (*Jesus the Christ* [Salt Lake City: The Church of Jesus Christ of Latter-day Saints, 1976], pp. 43, 82.) The seed of the woman is Jesus Christ. Thus the statement made to Satan that "[Jesus Christ] shall bruise thy head, and thou shalt bruise his heel" (Moses 4:21), becomes a clear declaration that good will triumph.

Before good can triumph, the man and the woman must suffer the consequences of their actions. They must pass their mortal test. God explained the conditions that would befall them. First the woman was told, "I will greatly multiply thy sorrow and thy conception. In sorrow thou shalt bring forth children" (Moses 4:22).

Paul adds: "And Adam was not deceived, but the woman being deceived was in the transgression. Notwithstanding she shall be saved in childbearing, if they continue in faith and charity and holiness with sobriety." (1 Timothy 2:14-15.)

The man was told: "Because thou hast hearkened unto the voice of thy wife, and hast eaten of the fruit of the tree of which I commanded thee, saying—Thou shalt not eat of it, cursed shall be the ground for thy sake; in sorrow shalt thou eat of it all the days of thy life. Thorns also, and thistles shall it bring forth to thee, and thou shalt eat the herb of the field. By the sweat of thy face shalt thou eat bread, until thou shalt return unto the ground—for thou shalt surely die—for out of it wast thou taken: for dust thou wast, and unto dust shalt thou return." (Moses 4:23-25.)

Too often we read "because thou hast hearkened unto the voice of thy wife . . . cursed shall be the ground. . . ." and conclude that it was bad for Adam to hearken to his wife. While it cannot be denied that thorns, thistles, weeds, and sweat are indeed a curse—and all of us who have lived have felt the consequences of this curse—we should also remember that by enduring the curse well Adam and Eve and all of us receive many blessings, as is the case with almost all curses and trials that we endure. In the end, this consequence was for Adam's sake, for his good, and was a blessing. Therefore one possible meaning included in this verse is, "Because thou hast hearkened unto the voice of thy wife, thou shalt be blessed."

In Moses 4:21 it is recorded that the Lord placed enmity between Satan and the woman. Could this explain why women by nature tend to be more spiritual than men? As a wife who has natural inclinations for spiritual things encourages and desires the spiritual, isn't a husband blessed who hearkens to her voice? Just because the husband is given the governmental role to preside does not mean that he cannot benefit by counseling with his wife. Indeed, both parties are benefited when her counsel is sought.

Although the consequences vary, in the account both Adam and Eve are told that they will have sorrow. Neither of them is singled out. Each is to be required to suffer the consequences of his or her actions. But the consequences actually become a blessing to them and their posterity, a means to bring them back into God's presence and to make them gods.

There has been much discussion about what is meant by the words "in sorrow thou shalt bring forth children." Some claim it means "into a world of sorrow." President Spencer W. Kimball said, "I wonder if those who translated the Bible might have used the term *distress* instead of sorrow." ("The Blessings and Responsibilities of Womanhood," *Ensign,* March 1976, p. 72.)

The dictionary says that sorrow is pain or distress of mind because of loss, injury, or misfortune. Certainly part of the sorrow they found themselves in was because of their loss and misfortune at having fallen from the presence of God. They would also bring children into the same distress and would toil to provide the necessities of life amid that same distress or loss.

In addition the woman was told, "And thy desire shall be to thy husband, and he shall rule over thee" (Genesis 3:16). Some people have interpreted this to be a commandment, but in context with both the verse and the surrounding verses it appears to be a description of the consequences of the Fall. In verses 14 and 15 the Lord tells the serpent what is going to happen to him because of what he did—he will be cursed above all cattle, etc. Verses 16 through 19 contain descriptions of consequences that will affect the man and woman. First the woman is told: "I will greatly multiply thy sorrow," and so on. Then Adam is told that because he has eaten of the tree the ground will be cursed, thorns and thistles will come, and he will have to toil all the days of his life.

None of the other things mentioned are commandments. All six verses contain descriptions of consequences. Therefore the statement that "thy desire shall be to thy husband, and he shall rule over thee," might well describe a condition in which women will desire and long for the "onement" and unity enjoyed before the Fall, while men will forget the shared relationship and instead desire to dominate and control, to be over the woman instead of one with her. Throughout history we have seen this happen as some men have tried to dominate and control both wives and women in general. But control and power struggles and unrighteous dominion are the opposite of everything Jesus Christ stood for and lived for.

The need to establish the line of governmental authority whereby men preside did not come until after the Fall and is a commandment separate from this description of consequences. With the Fall came chaos and the need for a system to bring about order. To fill that need men were given the responsibility to preside in the home and in the Church, which we will talk about in more detail later. Prior to the Fall, however, Adam and Eve existed as a

unit while at the same time maintaining separate but equal iden-
tities.

A Name for the Woman

Finally, after all their days in the garden and apparently at the
time of the expulsion from the garden, the woman was given a
name. It seems to be symbolic of the fact that they were no longer
one and would need to work to return to that state. Adam named
his wife Eve, "because she was the mother of all living; and thus
have I, the Lord God, called the first of all women, which are
many" (Moses 4:26). In Hebrew writings Eve's name is rendered
Chavvah, which means life-giver. It is significant that Adam called
Eve the mother of *all* living (not just the mother of all mankind, but
the mother of all living) before she ever had children. At the time
he names her the mother of all living, the only living beings besides the two of them are animals. We do not know exactly all that
is meant or implied by "mother of all living," but we do know that
by partaking of the forbidden fruit Eve initiated the change from an
immortal Edenic state to the mortal state we now call life. Perhaps
the name "mother of all living" has reference to this "birth" process.

We learn from what Adam named Eve, but what Adam does
not name Eve is also significant. He does not name her anything to
do with himself. He does not name her "my help meet" or "my
servant" or "the mother of my children." The choice of name indicates that Eve was recognized as a separate individual with a
mission and talents and that their oneness would come about by
adding to each other, not by becoming the same thing.

Together in Work and Trials

God clothed both Adam and Eve in coats of skins to protect
them and expelled them from the Garden of Eden to make a new
home for themselves in the lone and dreary world; a temporal
world they had brought about by partaking of the forbidden fruit.
And "Adam began to till the earth, and to have dominion over all
the beasts of the field, and to eat his bread by the sweat of his

brow, as I the Lord had commanded him. And Eve, also, his wife, did labor with him" (Moses 5:1).

Speaking of Eve and this verse, President Marion G. Romney said: "In their valiant, lonely struggle for a livelihood, this noble woman did labor with her husband. The word *with* as here used is very significant. It means more than physical labor. It connotes a common purpose, understanding, cooperation, and love." (Conference Report, Mexico City Area Conference 1977, p. 16.)

After the expulsion from the garden, Adam and Eve's days of trial began. They were faced with the task each of us is faced with: finding their way back to God. To do that they would have to re-establish the triangular Eden relationship with Deity, which required that they become whole and complete as a couple. Satan didn't want them to accomplish that now any more than he did while they were in the garden. Nor does Satan want any man and woman to become true counterparts. That is why he aims some of his most treacherous evils at the marriage relationship.

"All Things . . . Shall Work Together for Your Good"

One extremely important yet much overlooked fact of the creation story is that when people have righteous desires and intentions, the adversity Satan afflicts them with actually redounds to their good if they endure it well. As the scriptures tell us, "*all things wherewith you have been afflicted shall work together for your good*" (D&C 98:3, italics added). For Adam and Eve the Fall and its subsequent consequences and afflictions became a great blessing that led to their salvation. As we read, they even expressed thanks for that blessing.

In our own lives as we attempt to establish righteous relationships, Satan will be working hard to thwart our efforts just as he did the efforts of our first parents. If we endure faithfully, however, the things that curse and afflict us will be the very things that assist us in our quest for salvation. But we must do our part to turn the afflictions into blessings. The Lord promises: "Search diligently, pray always, and be believing, and all things shall work together for your good, if ye walk uprightly and remember the covenant wherewith ye have covenanted one with another" (D&C 90:24).

Who Should Be Head

A meeting I once attended became filled with examples of the struggles and frustrations in marriage. Story followed story of tyranny on the part of husbands, of nagging, belittling wives, of domestic power struggles, and of people honestly striving to set up the proper relationship but somehow missing the mark. People gave their interpretations of who should fulfill which role and how things should be done and the conversation grew more and more heated until one man who had listened quietly to the whole debate said, "If God isn't the head of a marriage, it doesn't matter who is." That is one of the most significant things we learn from the creation story. Adam and Eve fulfilled their destiny by letting God be their head, not by exercising power or control over each other.

One of the great tests of mortality is to see if man and woman can become complete and whole. The only way to accomplish that is to return to the triangular Eden relationship of man, woman, and God that Adam and Eve enjoyed before the Fall and re-established after the Fall.

He created man, male and female, after his own image
and in his own likeness, created he them.

—D&C 20:18

CHAPTER 3

In the Image of God

*A*fter speaking about the scriptures at a Relief Society meeting, I noticed a sister join the people talking with me. She seemed anxious to share something but kept falling to the back as others joined the group. Finally, when we were alone, tears filled her eyes as she said: "I've always hated the scriptures. The prophet tells us to read them, but every time I do I get the feeling God doesn't like women."

The words startled me, not just because of her distress but because this kind of incorrect perception makes a good marriage almost impossible. I assured her that God loves his daughters as much as he does his sons, and we discussed a few examples of his love and some of the problems that contribute to this kind of misunderstanding, such as the inadequacies of language.

Male Pronoun Includes Female

The English language does not have a third person singular pronoun that means both he and she. Where both male and female

are intended, the male pronoun is used even if the reference includes females, as in the sentence, "Each person must decide
whether he will be righteous." Even more confusing is the fact that
the word *man* is often used to mean mankind, which includes
women.

In addition, Elder Orson Pratt said that in the pure language
the name of God is *Ahman*, the Son of God is *Son Ahman*, the
name of men is *Sons Ahman*, and angels are *Anglo-man* (see *Journal
of Discourses* 2:342). According to this, even some designations of
the word *Sons* in the pure language include the daughters of God.
So when reading the scriptures, one must keep in mind Joseph
Smith's statement: "And now dear and well beloved brethren—
and when we say brethren, we mean those who have continued
faithful in Christ, men, women and children. . . ." (*Teachings of the
Prophet Joseph Smith,* comp. Joseph Fielding Smith [Salt Lake City:
Deseret Book Company, 1976], pp. 128–29.)

In God's Image—Male and Female

When we read the scriptures with these things in mind, it is
more obvious that God loves his daughters. And there is much
more. The daughters of God play a significant and necessary part
in the Father's great, eternal plan. At the time Adam and Eve were
created, God explained: "And I, God, created man in mine own
image, in the image of mine Only Begotten created I him; male and
female created I them. And I, God, blessed them, and said unto
them: Be fruitful, and multiply, and replenish the earth, and subdue it, and have dominion over the fish of the sea, and over the
fowl of the air, and over every living thing that moveth upon the
earth." (Moses 2:27–28.)

Latter-day prophets have elaborated on this scripture. President Joseph F. Smith explained: "No man will ever enter there [the
celestial kingdom] until he has consummated his mission; *for we
have come here to be conformed to the likeness of God.* He made us in
the beginning in his own image and in his own likeness, and he
made us male and female. We never could be in the image of God
if we were not both male and female." (*Gospel Doctrine* [Salt Lake
City: Deseret Book Company, 1977], p. 276, italics added.)

President Joseph Fielding Smith said: "Neither the man nor the woman were capable of filling the measure of their creation alone. The union of the two was required to complete man in the image of God." (*Doctrines of Salvation*, comp. Bruce R. McConkie, 3 vols. [Salt Lake City: Bookcraft, 1954-56], 2:70.)

"From the beginning of the creation" the Savior taught, "God made them male and female. For this cause shall a man leave his father and mother, and cleave to his wife; and they twain shall be one flesh: so then they are no more twain, but one flesh. What therefore God hath joined together, let no man put asunder." (Mark 10:6-9.) Paul added, "Nevertheless neither is the man without the woman, neither the woman without the man, in the Lord" (1 Corinthians 11:11).

In God's eternal plan neither the woman nor the man can receive exaltation alone. To reach exaltation each female must unite with a male and each male must unite with a female in celestial marriage. The couple sealed together as a unit can then progress to godhood. Those who do not have this opportunity in this life will, if worthy, be given the chance later. When it happens is not important. What is important is living worthily so that it can happen.

Balance Between Male and Female

Throughout the scriptures the balance between male and female is stressed repeatedly, both directly and indirectly. Paul tells us, "For as the woman is of the man, even so is the man also by the woman; but all things of God" (1 Corinthians 11:12). The woman is of the man—she was created from man's rib to be his help meet while they perform their mortal mission; and every man came forth from a woman and owes his mortal life to a mother. We see this stressed again by Paul: "But when the fulness of the time was come, God sent forth his Son, made of a woman, made under the law" (Galatians 4:4). The sentence could have easily ended after "sent forth his Son," but it would not then have stressed the important part Mary played in the birth of the Savior.

There is further significance in this delicate balance of male and female. In modern revelation the sun is proclaimed as *he* and the moon as *she* (D&C 88:45; see also 2 Nephi 23:10), and over thirty times in scripture the earth is characterized as female. In three verses (2 Nephi 9:7; Mosiah 2:26; Mormon 6:15) the earth is called "mother earth." Alma personified justice and mercy thus: "For behold, justice exerciseth all *his* demands, and also mercy claimeth all which is *her* own; and thus, none but the truly penitent are saved" (Alma 42:24, italics added). Several times the Lord uses the words *he* and *she* to describe two inanimate things or principles that even though separate must work in tandem to fulfill God's purposes, just as men and women must work in tandem to fulfill his purposes.

In the Mosaic law the burnt offering was a male animal without blemish. This had to be a male animal because it was symbolic of Jesus Christ and the atonement that he would make. But in Leviticus 4:28; 4:32; and 5:6 it tells us that the offering to be made by one of the common people who had sinned in ignorance had to be a female sheep or goat. Thus offerings could be either male or female, as prescribed, but always they had to be without blemish. Again we see the balance and the same emphasis: not all offerings were male, not all offerings were female; but all offerings had to be without defect. This balance and intermixing of "he" and "she," "his" and "her," and male and female is found throughout all the instructions, teachings, and symbolism God has given us.

It is not just because of balance that this is important. The work of the plan of salvation is to bring all things into one, to bring about unity or "onement"; "onement" of each individual's body and spirit, "onement" of a husband and a wife, "onement" of the couple with Jesus Christ and "onement" of Christ with the Father. Thus the concepts of maleness and femaleness are fundamental to the gospel of Jesus Christ. It is only by understanding this balance and the importance of reconciling male and female that we can progress toward salvation.

To Ensure Order Everyone Is to Submit

As we analyze the plan Father has established through his Son, we discover that in all things order reigns. Without order there would be chaos and no hope for salvation. Imagine what a ward would be like if it had no administrative structure. Nothing important could be accomplished. So it is in the kingdom of God. "But I would have you know," said Paul, "that the head of every man is Christ; and the head of the woman is the man; and the head of Christ is God" (1 Corinthians 11:3). This is the governmental order of the priesthood. The Father presides over Christ; Christ presides over man; and man presides over woman. Everyone must submit himself to someone else. Christ does submit to God; now man must submit to Christ, and woman to Christ and to a righteous man in order for them to become one in God. But none of that can happen unless each individual first subjects the body to the spirit. Thus man, woman, and God become one in light and truth by attending to their separate responsibilities.

It is important to realize that many of us have accepted the world's negative connotation for the concept of submission. In the gospel context submission means becoming one with God. We submit our will to God's will and thereby become one with him. It is the only way "onement" with God can come about. We can only give ourselves to him; otherwise he cannot and will not take us. With this understanding it is easy to see that submission does not mean that man is superior to woman. Neither does it mean that man can demand that a woman submit. Submission must be freely given; otherwise it is not submission but slavery.

A bishop is the head of the ward, but is he superior to the rest of the members of the ward? No. He is the designated person to receive revelation for the operation of the ward. The question of order and the concept of submission have nothing to do with superiority or personal righteousness. So why do men and women sometimes fall into the trap of thinking that God favors his sons simply because they have been called to preside?

No scriptural basis exists for such thought. Many of the things that have tended to establish feelings of male superiority are cultural traditions which have no validation in the scriptures. For instance, President Joseph Fielding Smith pointed out one such restriction imposed by our traditions: "According to modern custom, it is the place of the man to take the initiative in the matter of a marriage contract. Women are, by force of such custom, kept in reserve and whether it be right or wrong for a woman to take the lead and offer a proposal of marriage, she feels, and she knows that the public would also feel, that she was acting in a forward and unbecoming manner. This is all wrong, but nevertheless it is the fact.

The responsibility therefore rests upon the man." (*Doctrines of Salvation* 2:76–77.)

Some customs and traditions are harmless, but others actually keep us from achieving the "onement" and spiritual state of unity we could achieve. Ideas such as "Men don't change diapers" or "Women can't handle finances" may be transmitted to us by tradition, but they are not valid.

The Lord tells us that families are important and that both fathers and mothers have responsibility to care for and teach their children. They also are to magnify their callings in the Church. We should be very careful that we do not let cultural traditions keep us from the duties and joys of our divine destiny or from helping our spouse fill the measure of his or her creation.

Throughout the scriptures we find that the only favoritism shown occurs not by God choosing or not choosing men or women but by men and women choosing or not choosing God. Sometimes, however, especially in our Old Testament reading, we misinterpret what is going on. The Mosaic law was a case law approach to teaching. This meant that the Lord gave the people specific instructions on what to do and how to do it; the people were then to learn the principles from the symbolism of the specifics. Today the Lord has reversed that process. He teaches us principles and expects us to determine the specifics.

When we understand this we learn several principles from the Mosaic law that help us to recognize how our Father in Heaven intended the balance between male and female and priesthood government or order to work. Numbers chapter 30 explains that when a man swore a vow with the Lord he was bound to do whatever he had promised. If a woman made a vow with the Lord the vow was binding unless her father or husband disallowed it on the day of first hearing it. If the father or husband disallowed the vow, the Lord would forgive her for not fulfilling the vow. If on the first hearing, however, the man concerned did not disapprove, the vow was binding upon her and he could no longer disapprove it. Women who were widows or divorced were bound by every oath they made and were not subject to any review.

This may at first seem as if the man controlled the woman, but there is one important stipulation. If a man disallowed the vow, he placed himself in the position of total responsibility. If the vow was a righteous vow and in accordance with the Lord's will, then he would be held responsible for its nonfulfillment. The man presides to assure order, but with that comes the burden of responsibility. The woman answers to her father or husband, but the father or husband in turn answers to Jesus Christ. The call to preside is not a call to indulge one's selfish desires or to be served. Instead the call to preside is a call to serve. It is a call of responsibility to assure that all is done in righteousness and that order prevails.

It is also important to understand that the vows Old Testament women made with their Heavenly Father were not concerned with trivial matters. Hannah made a vow with the Lord that if he would send her a son, she would give the boy back to the Lord. Her husband, Elkanah, upheld the vow; and after their firstborn son, Samuel, was weaned, he was given to Eli to be reared and to serve in the temple. (See 1 Samuel 1; 2:1–21.)

The beauty of the gospel plan is that both God's sons and daughters can deal directly with him. Even though the man presides as to government, a woman's access to her Father in Heaven is in no way limited; nor is it different from a man's. God places no restrictions on a woman's prayers. While maintaining order on the earth, his system allows a woman to make vows and covenants directly with him.

God Treats Men and Women Equally

We see more of God's encouragement for the spiritual development of both his sons and daughters in Numbers 6:2, where we learn that a man or a woman could make a vow to be a Nazarite. A Nazarite was a person who entered a consecrated state by his or her own or a parent's vow and who lived a stricter law for a designated period of time or for a lifetime. The Nazarites did not drink wine or strong drink, did not allow a razor to touch their hair, and did not go near a dead body, not even that of a parent or loved one. The intent was to dedicate or consecrate oneself to the Lord, to do his work, and to live closer to him.

In Moses' time when a tabernacle was built to worship the Lord and carry on the sacred ordinances, "the children of Israel brought a willing offering unto the Lord, every man and woman, whose heart made them willing to bring for all manner of work, which the Lord had commanded to be made by the hand of

Moses" (Exodus 35:29). From this we see that the Lord wants all his children to help in his work. Gender does not determine favor with God; purity of heart does. God is no respecter of persons; and while man and woman are different, they are equally important and share equally in the blessings of the gospel. These blessings— such as the ordinances of the temple, baptism, the gift of the Holy Ghost, and the sacrament—are available to males and females alike. As Alma taught, the Lord "imparteth his word by angels unto men, yea, not only men but women also" (Alma 32:23).

We find in the Mosaic law that when the ordinances and practices were not alike, there were equivalents for men and women. Most of us are aware of the covenant of circumcision. Circumcision was for males and was deeply symbolic.

> The organ of the body that produces seed and brings about physical birth is the organ on which the token of the covenant was made. The organ of spiritual rebirth, however, is the heart (see 3 Nephi 9:20). Thus, when a person was circumcised it signified that while he had been born into the covenant, he need not be baptized until he became accountable before the Lord. But spiritual circumcision, or the circumcision of the heart, must take place once one becomes accountable or one is not considered as true Israel. (*Old Testament Student Manual, Genesis–2 Samuel* [Salt Lake City: The Church of Jesus Christ of Latter-day Saints, 1980], p. 69.)

The law of purification as explained in Leviticus 12 and 15 was the female equivalent of circumcision. "Circumcision witnesses to the fact that man's hope is not in generation but in regeneration, and the witness of the ceremony of the purification of women is the same" (Rousas John Rushdoony, *The Institutes of Biblical Law* [The Presbyterian and Reformed Publishing Company, 1973], p. 43). The law stated that if a woman gave birth to a son, she was separated from the congregation for seven days and then had an additional thirty-three days of purification for a total of forty days. If she bore a daughter the days of separation were fourteen and the days of purification were sixty-six for a total of eighty days. At the end of the days of purification the mother was ritually washed and presented at the temple, where she offered a yearling lamb or, if she was poor, two pigeons or doves, to be sacrificed by the priest.

The interesting thing is that the Mosaic law also stipulated that a male child was to be circumcised when eight days old. In addition a firstborn son was presented in the temple when forty days old. If the purification time was the same for a son as for a daughter the mother could not have attended the presentation as Mary did when Jesus was presented in the temple. This, however, is not the reason for the difference in the time of separation. When a woman had a baby, she underwent a forty-day period of uncleanness and purification for herself. Then, if the baby was male he was circumcised; if the baby was female, the forty-day ritual period was doubled. As Rushdoony seems to be saying in the quotation above, the circumcision of the male baby and the additional forty-day separation for the female baby symbolically declared the need for spiritual rebirth for the child and all mankind.

To really understand the symbolism, however, we need to understand the dual significance of purification. Under the Mosaic law there were two uses for terms such as *unclean* and *impure*. One involved personal impurity and the other moral impurity. Moral impurity was sin committed by the person; it required repentance and purification from the sin. Personal impurity referred to the Fall and the unclean and impure state we all find ourselves in because of mortality. This required a purification or separation from the world, or from the carnal, natural, and sensual.

Blood is a symbol of mortality and the impurity all of us encounter simply by being born. Therefore the purification after childbirth and menstruation was a ritual (as was circumcision) symbolizing that a woman must separate herself from the world or wash away the influence of the world in order to be born into the kingdom of God.

Prophetesses

We learn more about women from the five righteous prophetesses mentioned in the Bible. The first was Miriam, Moses' sister, who appears to have been the "General Relief Society President" of her time because of the way she leads the women (see Exodus 15:20–21). The next prophetess mentioned was Deborah, one of the judges of Israel, who helped deliver Israel from its enemies. Huldah was a prophetess who prophesied of King Josiah's life and death (see 2 Kings 22). Isaiah's wife is also mentioned as being a prophetess (Isaiah 8:3), but she is not called by name. These four are found in the Old Testament and there is one more in the New Testament. This fifth prophetess is Anna, a devout widow of about eighty-four years who prayed and fasted much, and who "departed not from the temple" (Luke 2:37); Anna recognized and testified that Jesus was the Christ while he was still an infant.

Elder Orson Pratt said, "There never was a genuine Christian Church unless it had Prophets and Prophetesses" (*Journal of Discourses* 18:171). A prophetess is the female counterpart of a prophet. "In a general sense a prophet is anyone who has a testimony of Jesus Christ by the Holy Ghost" (LDS Bible Dictionary, p. 754; see also Revelation 19:10). Besides the women specifically identified as prophetesses, women such as Mary the mother of Jesus and Elisabeth the mother of John the Baptist certainly fit the definition of a prophetess.

Other women of the Old and New Testaments also received revelation and heavenly messengers from the Lord. A few examples are Rebekah, Samson's mother, and Hagar, who each received revelation to direct their lives. Again these women were chosen not because of or in spite of gender, but because they were worthy and because revelation was needed for them to fulfill their missions in life.

Moses exclaimed, "Would God that all the Lord's people were prophets, and that the Lord would put his spirit upon them!" (Numbers 11:29.) In the latter days Brigham Young said:

> My knowledge is, if you will follow the teachings of Jesus Christ and his Apostles, as recorded in the New Testament, every man and woman will be put in possession of the Holy Ghost; every person will become a Prophet, Seer, and Revelator, and an expounder of truth. They will know things that are, that will be, and that have been. They will understand things in heaven, things on the earth, and things under the earth, things of time, and things of eternity, according to their several callings and capacities. (*Journal of Discourses* 1:243.)

God wants his sons and his daughters to be prophets and prophetesses for themselves and those under their care, but it is each son and each daughter who must choose to receive this blessing.

In the rededication prayer of the St. George Temple in 1975, Spencer W. Kimball referred to prophetesses and holy women: "We again ask Thy blessing on the women in all the land, that they may accomplish the measure of their creation as daughters of God, Thy offspring. Let the blessings of Sarah, Huldah, Hannah, Anna and Mary, the mother of the Son of God, bless these women to fulfill their duties as did Mary, our beloved mother of Thy Son, and let the power and satisfactions of the prophetesses and all holy women rest upon these mothers as they move forward to fulfill their destinies." (*Church News*, November 15, 1975, p. 7.)

The phrase, "power and satisfactions of the prophetesses," carries with it a great deal of meaning. One of the greatest powers of a prophet or a prophetess is to be able to know what the Lord wants done and to have the ability to do it. This could lead each of us to ask several personal questions that have great impact on a marriage. Can there be any real satisfaction in life if we do not do what the Lord wants us to do? Can the ways of the world offer men or women any lasting satisfaction? Are we looking in the right places for our satisfaction? Do we have the power of the prophetesses and the prophets?

Women in Scripture

One of the great chapters of scripture dealing with women is Proverbs 31. Starting with verse 10 we find a long list of things that make a virtuous woman. According to this list a woman should be strong, wise, spiritual, industrious, knowledgeable, compassionate, and loving. In verse 23 it says that "her husband is known in the gates, when he sitteth among the elders of the land." The last verse adds, "let [the woman's] own works praise her in the gates." The Lord never intended for a woman to hover in a man's shadow; instead she is to be known for her own good works.

There are few discussions of men and women in the gospel context that don't eventually come around to Paul. Some of the things Paul said seem to be anti-woman unless one understands the context in which they were given. For instance, the heading to 1 Corinthians 7 in the LDS edition of the Bible indicates that Paul is speaking to those called on missions. If we were to take the instructions given at the Missionary Training Center and hide them away for a thousand years, then compile them with other scripture and give it to people, the readers would have trouble understanding things such as: "You are not to telephone, write to, or accept calls or letters from anyone of the opposite sex;" or "Never live where single people of the opposite sex live" (Missionary Handbook, 1986, p. 21). So it is with the instructions Paul gave to the Corinthians.

Other misunderstandings regarding Paul's sayings can be attributed to translation errors. In 1 Corinthians 14:35 Paul instructs, "it is a shame for women to speak in the church." These words were changed in the Joseph Smith Translation to read, "it is a shame for women to *rule* in the church."

In Philippians 4:3 Paul says, "And I intreat thee also, true yokefellow, help those women which laboured with me in the gospel." Here we find another testimony that the Lord calls women to help in the Church. In addition, in the Greek that the New Testament was translated from the term *yokefellow* was an idiom which meant an associate, someone you were yoked with through purpose or friendship. Some Bible scholars maintain that the term *true yokefellow* was only used to refer to a spouse. This makes sense in this verse. It is logical that Paul would call on his wife, his true counterpart, to help the women, much as a mission president might today ask his wife to take special heed of the sister missionaries.

Perhaps the greatest testimony of a woman's importance, however, is not found in what is said in scripture but what is *not* said. There are few places in scripture in which a woman is specifically told, "This does not apply to you." In modern revelation we are told: "Seek ye earnestly the best gifts, always remembering for what they are given; for verily I say unto you, they are given for the benefit of those who love me and keep all my commandments, and him that seeketh so to do; that all may be benefited that seek or that ask of me, that ask and not for a sign that they may consume it upon their lusts" (D&C 46:8–9).

The section goes on to list many gifts of the Spirit such as the testimony of Jesus, faith to believe, wisdom, knowledge, faith to be healed, faith to heal others, working of miracles, ability to prophesy, discerning of spirits, speaking in tongues, and interpretation of tongues. Clearly these gifts are given by the Spirit according to worthiness and faith—not according to gender. Husbands and wives should help each other to obtain the best gifts and should realize that they will be held accountable if they hinder their spouse from developing spiritual gifts or talents.

Fulfilling Pre-Assigned Missions

Every man and woman has duties in life that he or she needs to perform. President Kimball has admonished: "Remember, in the world before we came here, faithful women were given certain assignments while faithful men were foreordained to certain priesthood tasks. While we do not now remember the particulars, this does not alter the glorious reality of what we once agreed to." (*The Teachings of Spencer W. Kimball,* ed. Edward L. Kimball [Salt Lake City: Bookcraft, 1982], p. 316.) Each man and woman should pray and ponder and seek the Spirit to know what the duties of his or her mission in life are and then seek the gifts that will best help him or her to perform that mission. Every husband and wife should also pray and ponder and seek the Spirit so that he or she will understand the duties of his or her spouse. Only with such understanding can we truly assist our counterparts to best perform their missions in life.

Heavenly Mother

Of all the teachings, all the doctrines and examples in the scriptures, we find nothing more beautiful or more significant for the sons and daughters of God than the scripture we began with: "And I, God, created man in mine own image, in the image of mine Only Begotten created I him; male and female created I them" (Moses 2:27). What is the image of God? Male and female. A man alone cannot be a god. A woman alone cannot be a god. Together, man and woman united in righteousness—the couple— become gods. Therefore, a good woman becomes one of the keys to a man's salvation; and a good man becomes one of the keys to a woman's salvation.

When we understand this important concept it is not hard to comprehend why we see the balance between male and female stressed throughout the scriptures. But the question continues to be asked, "If we are in the image of God, male *and* female, why don't we hear anything about our Heavenly Mother?'' Eliza R. Snow's great hymn "O My Father," asks the question: "In the heav'ns are parents single?" The hymn answers: "No, the thought makes reason stare! / Truth is reason; truth eternal / Tells me I've a mother there." (*Hymns*, no. 292.)

But more than just reason allows us to know of a Heavenly Mother; our understanding that to be a god the male and female must become one helps us realize that sometimes when the term *God* is used it includes our Heavenly Mother. Heavenly Father and Mother are one, sealed together eternally. A verse such as "God loveth a cheerful giver" (1 Corinthians 9:7) means to me not just my Heavenly Father, but also my Heavenly Mother. We must be careful, however, that we do not interpret every use of the word *God* as meaning both of them. Here on earth we have separate duties and responsibilities; and, once again, reason would lead us to believe that in the celestial kingdom fathers and mothers also have duties and responsibilities separate from one another.

In the gospel of Jesus Christ the Lord calls exalted men and exalted women gods with no distinction as to gender. We do not use the word *goddess*. Elder Bruce R. McConkie explained: "Exaltation grows out of the eternal union of a man and his wife. Of those whose marriage endures in eternity, the Lord says, 'Then shall *they* be gods' (D&C 132:20); that is, each of them, the man and the woman, will be a god. As such they will rule over their dominions forever." (*Mormon Doctrine*, 2nd ed. [Salt Lake City: Bookcraft, 1966], p. 613.) Perhaps this once again stresses the oneness and unity of the couple. In the beginning they were called Adam (Moses 6:9); and if they are true and faithful, in the end they will be called god.

The word *El*, by which God is known in the Hebrew language, teaches us more of this concept. In Hebrew *im* is the plural ending. *El* (which means might or strength) is used to designate "the divine being." The plural form, *Elohim*, means "the divine being*s*."

We recognize also that prior to the time of the Savior many Israelites fell away from the truth, even adopting heathen practices. At least one king took over the temple and changed rituals and furnishings (see 2 Kings 16:17). Prophets such as Nehemiah and Malachi spoke out against such changes and tried to restore truth, but the majority of the people did not respond. It appears that this falling away from truth introduced traditions and changes that also affected women's status.

After the time of Christ the Great Apostasy brought such doctrines as celibacy and male supremacy to the apostate church. We have no way of knowing whether or how many references to marriage and woman were purposely removed from or altered in Bible records (see 1 Nephi 13:21-28). In recently discovered ancient documents such as the Dead Sea Scrolls and the Nag Hammadi manuscripts women have more prominence than they do in the Bible. This leads some to believe that in the scriptures deletions and changes concerning women and our Heavenly Mother have been made. We do not know for certain what occurred.

We do know that if our Heavenly Father has intentionally avoided teaching us about our Heavenly Mother he has a good reason for doing so. Some have speculated about his reasons, but these reasons really don't matter. If he has chosen not to tell us, and if we believe in an omnipotent, omniscient, loving God, we know we can trust in his wisdom.

Whatever the reason for her not being mentioned, we know we have a Heavenly Mother. We can even find at least one possible indirect reference to her. The Spirit of the Lord appeared to Nephi and showed him many things that would occur upon the earth. "And he [the Spirit of the Lord] said unto me: Behold, the virgin whom thou seest is the mother of the Son of God, *after the manner of the flesh*" (1 Nephi 11:18, italics added). This could merely be a pattern of speaking, but it could also be a qualification indicating which mother. The Spirit could have stopped after "mother of the Son of God," and the meaning would have been clear. Therefore the designation of which mother may have been given to help us more fully understand that this was not Jesus' mother after the manner of the spirit, or his Heavenly Mother, but his mother after the manner of the flesh. If there was no mother of the spirit there would have been no need for this distinction.

In summary, we may not know much about our Heavenly Mother but we do know she exists. In 1909 the First Presidency said: "All men and women are in the similitude of the universal Father and Mother, and are literally the sons and daughters of Deity" (*Messages of the First Presidency*, comp. James R. Clark, 6 vols. [Salt Lake City: Bookcraft, 1965-75], 4:203).

When men and women really understand the plan of salvation they cannot doubt God's love or concern for either his sons or his daughters. From the beginning we were created in God's image, male and female. To maintain order in the kingdom, God established a system of government. To his sons God gave the stewardship over the life-giving ordinances of the priesthood. To his daughters God gave the stewardship over life. Both are great gifts. Both are tremendous responsibilities. Both are necessary for salvation. A man who demeans womanhood or motherhood in any way will incur the displeasure of God. A woman who demeans manhood or priesthood in any way will incur the displeasure of God. Mutual respect is a necessary foundation for a good marriage relationship.

The scriptures are full of teachings that help us understand that the great plan of salvation was established to give both God's sons and daughters all the experiences and help they need in order to find their way back to him. If we read and study not only with our minds but also with our hearts, we can feel as well as know how very much our Father loves us—that is, loves each of the spouses. This knowledge enhances our love, respect, and devotion for our counterpart, deepens our commitment to marriage, and molds us more completely into the image of God.

Behold, I am he who was prepared from the foundation of the world to redeem my people. Behold, I am Jesus Christ. I am the Father and the Son. In me shall all mankind have life, and that eternally, even they who shall believe on my name; and they shall become my sons and my daughters.

—*Ether 3:14*

CHAPTER 4

A Savior for Man and for Woman

*E*arly on a Sunday morning, before the sun dispersed the darkness, Mary Magdalene arrived at the sepulchre where her Lord had been entombed. As she drew near she found the soldiers gone and the sepulchre stone rolled away. Startled, Mary left the garden, found the Apostles Peter and John, and told them what she supposed had happened. "They have taken away the Lord out of the sepulchre, and we know not where they have laid him."

Peter and John ran back to the garden with Mary. John, arriving first, stopped outside the sepulchre, looked into the chamber, but saw only burial linen. When Peter arrived he entered the chamber, saw the linen, and noticed that the napkin which had been about the Savior's head was set aside in a place by itself.

Leaving the empty tomb, Peter and John returned to their homes; but Mary sat outside the sepulchre weeping. Through tear-filled eyes she peered once again into the sepulchre and saw two angels sitting, one where Jesus' head had lain and the other where his feet had been. She did not seem startled by them or their words: "Woman, why weepest thou?"

"Because they have taken away my Lord, and I know not where they have laid him."

As Mary turned back toward the garden, she saw a man standing nearby. "Woman, why weepest thou?" he asked, "Whom seekest thou?"

"Sir, if thou have borne him hence," Mary pleaded, assuming him to be the gardener, "tell me where thou hast laid him, and I will take him away."

He replied with one word—her name—to which Mary responded, "Rabboni!"

Quickly Jesus warned her, "Hold me not; for I am not yet ascended to my Father" (JST, John 20:17). Then he instructed Mary, "Go to my brethren, and say unto them, I ascend unto my Father, and your Father; and to my God, and your God."

Women in the Early Church

Concerning this account from John 20:1–17, Elder Bruce R. McConkie wrote:

> For reasons of his own, the Risen Lord singled out Mary Magdalene to be the first witness, in point of time, of his resurrection. She was the first mortal of all mortals ever to see a resurrected person. She saw his face and heard his voice, and she was commanded to tell the Twelve of the appearance and of the coming ascension when he would report to Him whose he was. Then, still in his own infinite wisdom, Jesus chose to appear to and be handled by a group of other women—all before he came even to Peter and the rest of the Twelve, all before his appearances to the hundreds of brethren who were privileged to see him before that day on the Mount of Olives when he ascended to reign on the right hand of Everlasting Power forever. (*The Mortal Messiah*, 4 vols. [Salt Lake City: Deseret Book Company, 1979–81], 4:265.)

Jesus did not appear first to Peter, who upon the Savior's death was the earthly head of the Church, or to his mother and brothers and sisters. He did not even appear to Mary just minutes before while Peter and John were still there. Instead Jesus showed himself just to Mary even before he had ascended to God.

Just as women were the first to know of Jesus' impending birth, they were first to know of his resurrection. In addition to this, the story is a testimony of the principles talked about in chapter 3. The Savior said, "I ascend unto my Father, and your Father; and to my God, and your God" (John 20:17). One wonders whether this might be one of the places where *God* means both Heavenly Father and Heavenly Mother; for logic and reason suggest that his Heavenly Mother would have been one of the first to greet her Son.

The accounts of the Resurrection in the books of John and Luke differ somewhat, so it is difficult to know exactly the sequence of events after the Resurrection, but it is clear that Jesus appeared to other women besides Mary Magdalene before he appeared to his Apostles. Luke tells us that Joanna, Mary the mother of Joses, Salome the mother of James and John, and other unnamed women went to the sepulchre with spices and ointments for the Savior's body, but they found the stone removed and the body gone. Two angels appeared to them saying, "Why seek ye the living among the dead?" (Luke 24:5.) The angels then sent the women to tell the disciples the wonderful news. As they went, Jesus appeared to them himself and again instructed them to tell his Apostles. Some of the Apostles—perhaps not yet having enough faith or perhaps still tied to cultural traditions that could not accept that women could be the first to see the resurrected Lord—listened, but the women's "words seemed to them as idle tales, and they believed them not" (Luke 24:11).

Of this account Elder Bruce R. McConkie wrote: "Jesus is using them [the sisters] and the fact of his resurrection to show the unity and oneness and equality of the man and the woman. 'Neither is the man without the woman, neither the woman without the man, in the Lord.' (1 Corinthians 11:11.) Together they form an eternal family unit; together they serve in the earthly kingdom; together they gain the spiritual stature to see visions and converse with those who abide beyond the veil." (*The Mortal Messiah*, 4:267.)

The Savior's life is a great testimony of the importance of balance between male and female in his gospel. Never in any of the Savior's teachings or in the things which he did is there any favoritism shown to males or females because of gender. This becomes even more profound when we realize that at the time the Savior lived the Jews had fallen into a state of apostasy. Instead of being respected as helps meet—counterparts, equals, that which completes and makes whole—women had become possessions. By the time Jesus was born women were segregated in the synagogues and discriminated against in culturally accepted practices. But Jesus did not follow cultural traditions. He treated women with great respect and impartially offered them his gospel. Elder James E. Talmage explained: "In our Lord's day the prevailing laxity in the matter of marital obligation had produced a state of appalling corruption in Israel; and woman, who by the law of God had been made a companion and partner with man, had become his slave. The world's greatest champion of woman and womanhood is Jesus the Christ." (*Jesus the Christ* [Salt Lake City: The Church of Jesus Christ of Latter-day Saints, 1976], pp. 474-75.)

Jesus taught women the gospel not just as part of a group or crowd but also as individuals. In the story of the Samaritan woman at the well, we often discuss how Jesus broke the cultural traditions in that he spoke with a Samaritan; but it was of equal significance that he taught a woman (see John 4:7-14).

In addition to teaching the women, Jesus did not confine himself to the male experience when illustrating the principles he was explaining. His teachings are full of women; women sewing, the widow giving her mite, ten virgins going to meet the bridegroom, women putting leaven in the bread, etc. Jesus' choice of examples was itself a testimony that it was important to him that the sisters also understand what he was teaching. And we know that they did understand, too. In the New Testament the term *disciple* means the righteous men *and* women who followed the Savior. "Now there was at Joppa a certain disciple named Tabitha, which by interpretation is called Dorcas: this woman was full of good works and almsdeeds which she did" (Acts 9:36).

On one occasion the publicans and sinners gathered to the Savior while the Pharisees and scribes murmured, "This man receiveth sinners, and eateth with them." The Savior replied with three parables. The first was the story of the good shepherd. "What man of you, having an hundred sheep, if he lose one of them, doth not leave the ninety and nine in the wilderness, and go after that which is lost, until he find it?" (Luke 15:4.) The second example is of the woman who sought the lost coin. It begins with the question, "Either what woman having ten pieces of silver, if she lose one piece, doth not light a candle, and sweep the house, and seek diligently till she find it?" (Luke 15:8.) The third example is the story of the prodigal son (see Luke 15:11-32).

We are all familiar with each of these stories, but when we look at them in context, we see more depth and meaning to them. Of these parables Elder Bruce R. McConkie said, "Jesus is the Shepherd who has come to save the 'little ones' who otherwise would be lost," and concerning the parable of the prodigal son, "the Father is God who endows all his children with talents, capacities, powers, and agency." (*Doctrinal New Testament Commentary*, 3 vols. [Salt Lake City: Bookcraft, 1965], 1:508, 511.)

Elder James E. Talmage said that the woman in the second parable "may be taken to represent" the Church (see *Jesus the Christ*, p. 456). Throughout the scriptures the Church is identified as female. It is significant that the Savior chose to symbolize the Church as a woman. The Prophet Joseph once corrected an interpretation of the beasts in the Revelation of John as representing the Kingdom of God on earth. He said, "I could not help laughing that God should take a figure of a beast to represent his kingdom consisting of Men. — To take a lesser figure to represent a greater." (*The Words of Joseph Smith*, comp. Andrew F. Ehat and Lyndon W. Cook [Provo, Utah: Religious Studies Center, Brigham Young University, 1980], p. 188.) Therefore, it is a great honor that Jesus chose to represent the Church as female. In addition, this parable seems to indicate that women as well as men should be involved in the work of "finding" lost souls and bringing them back into the kingdom.

Besides teaching women, Jesus also numbered Mary and Martha and other women among his closest friends. "Now Jesus loved Martha, and her sister, and Lazarus" (John 11:5). There are also references to the women who followed him from Galilee to Jerusalem, a distance of about seventy miles, to hear his teachings and to stay near him just before his death. Even in his final mortal moments the women were there. "And all his acquaintance, and the women that followed him from Galilee, stood afar off, beholding these things" (Luke 23:49). In these moments of agony, his last earthly instruction was concerning a woman, his mother, Mary. First Jesus spoke to her saying, "Woman, behold thy son!" Then turning to his apostle, John, Jesus said, "Behold thy mother!" John understood the Savior's message and reverenced Mary, for "from that hour that disciple took her unto his own home" (John 19:26-27).

Throughout the Savior's life he showed a deep respect for women. Never did Jesus send the women away. Never did he refuse to heal them or to minister to them. Never did he brush aside their concerns or their contributions. On one occasion his disciples even murmured when he did not do so:

> And Jesus being in Bethany, in the house of Simon the leper, as he sat at meat, there came a woman having an alabaster box of ointment of spikenard, very precious, and she brake the box, and poured the ointment on his head.
>
> There were some among the disciples who had indignation within themselves, and said, Why was this waste of the ointment made? for it might have been sold for more than three hundred pence, and have been given to the poor. And they murmured against her.
>
> And Jesus said unto them, Let her alone; why trouble ye her? For she hath wrought a good work on me.
>
> Ye have the poor with you always, and whensoever ye will, ye may do them good; but me ye have not always.
>
> She has done what she could, and this which she has done unto me, shall be had in remembrance in generations to come, wheresoever my gospel shall be preached; for verily she has come beforehand to anoint my body to the burying. (JST, Mark 14:4–8.)

The JST changes made in John 12:7 add to this account in Mark and help us understand the significance of what Mary was doing; something she obviously understood even though some of the other disciples did not. It reads: ''Then said Jesus, Let her alone; for she hath preserved this ointment until now, that she might anoint me in token of my burial.''

Jesus Embodied the Best Characteristics

Perhaps the most interesting aspect of Jesus' ministry and example to us, however, is the way he was a blend of the traditionally male and female traits in his own life. Cultures throughout the ages have formed philosophical designations of male and female characteristics. Traits such as weak, soft, quiet, frail, servant, timid, and small are traditionally classified as female, while traits such as strong, rough, loud, sturdy, master, bold, and big are classified as male. However, the Savior's life exemplified the best of both the male and female cultural values, so that his life was quite naturally a perfect balance between the two. Therefore he did not always act in a stereotypical male way. The circumstances and situation rather than his gender determined the response he gave. There were times such as the cleansing of the temple when he was strong and tough, bold, and probably loud. But there were also many occasions when he responded with softness, quietness, gentleness, and tears.

> When Jesus therefore saw [Mary] weeping, and the Jews also weeping which came with her, he groaned in the spirit, and was troubled, And said, Where have ye laid him?
> They said unto him, Lord, come and see.
> Jesus wept.
> Then said the Jews, Behold how he loved him! (John 11:33–36.)

One of the Savior's strengths was that instead of adapting himself to cultural traditions he adapted himself (he submitted) to the righteous designs of his Heavenly Father. He did not cultivate "male traits" or "female traits," but instead cultivated righteous traits. That is why Jesus Christ is not only the way and the model for the men of the Church but for the women also. There is only one way, and Jesus is that way. Some women bemoan the fact that there is no female model. They seek the wrong image. Male is not the model. Female is not the model. Righteousness is the model.

I was once telling a friend about a violinist I admire very much and how deeply he touches me every time he places bow to strings. "That is because he plays with the strength of a man and the emotion of a woman," she replied. "When the two come together there is always power." That might be considered one of the great lessons portrayed in the Savior's life. He incorporated all that was good into his life. If we are to emulate him we must do the same. Instead of building our lives or our marriages around stereotypes of what a man or a woman is or should be, we should adapt ourselves to circumstances, being strong or sweet or timid or bold as is required by the situation and the promptings of the Spirit. As counterparts we should also help and learn from each other so that we take on the strengths of our partner.

When we begin to catch the vision of this concept we begin to see more of the purposes of marriage. What better way to learn a strength than to live intimately with a person who possesses that strength, to see it firsthand day in and day out? Too often we take for granted our partner's strengths or even become jealous or annoyed that he or she can do something we can't. If we fall into this trap we deny ourselves one of the greatest blessings of marriage.

In other cases we excuse our own incorrect behavior by thinking that that's what a man or a woman is supposed to do. The Savior taught us differently. Instead of looking to cultural standards and traditions to determine our behavior, we need to look to the Savior.

On one occasion, Jesus corrected Martha for adhering too closely to a role that was dictated by tradition instead of the Spirit.

> Now it came to pass, as they went, that he entered into a certain village: and a certain woman named Martha received him into her house.
>
> And she had a sister called Mary, which also sat at Jesus' feet, and heard his word.
>
> But Martha was cumbered about much serving, and came to him, and said, Lord, dost thou not care that my sister hath left me to serve alone? bid her therefore that she help me.
>
> And Jesus answered and said unto her, Martha, Martha, thou art careful and troubled about many things:
>
> But one thing is needful: and Mary hath chosen that good part, which shall not be taken away from her. (Luke 10:38-42.)

Martha was caught in a web of traditional female duties. She was fretting and worrying about serving. Jesus was not telling Martha never to clean or cook or serve. Instead he was telling her that she must analyze each circumstance and fit her actions to the situation. She must set priorities based on eternal values and not be strapped to traditions that would keep her from the one needful thing. This is also a clear statement that study of the gospel of Jesus Christ is as important for a woman as it is for a man. In our own day President Spencer W. Kimball repeatedly encouraged "our sisters to be scholars of the scriptures as well as our men" ("Privileges and Responsibilities of Sisters," *Ensign,* November 1978, p. 102).

Jesus also warned us against other cultural traditions that can keep us from our eternal destiny. "But he that is greatest among you, let him be as the younger; and he that is chief, as he that doth serve. For whether is greater, he that sitteth at meat, or he that serveth, is not he that sitteth at meat? but I am among you as he that serveth." (Luke 22:26-27.) The Savior is talking about the cultural notion that the person served is the greatest person while the servant is the lesser person. There could even be deeper implications in these verses, because at the time of the Savior, some historians tell us, the women did not eat with the men. They served the men, and when the men had finished the women ate. Whatever the implication, the Savior aligned himself with the server and not with the one being served.

In addition to this, Jesus ministered to the little children even though they were not physically his own children. His example of serving and loving the children again falls on the female side of traditional values. One sister remarked that she felt certain that if the Savior were to come into an LDS building during meetings, he would go directly to the nursery.

Since the beginning of time, cultures have developed male-female traditions. Some cultures have been predominantly matriarchal; others have been predominantly patriarchal. In each the issue is power and control—the very things Satan wanted and that we fought against in the premortal life. The very reason we are on this earth is that we stood against one person controlling others. Jesus did not seek power in the premortal life or in his mortal life, instead he sought to serve. He recognized that the only real power is that which comes from God.

As husbands and wives we can learn much from this. Instead of trying to control each other through force or emotional manipulation we should seek to deal with each other righteously. Wouldn't mortal life as well as marriage be much simpler if we stopped thinking in terms of the male and female roles and thought instead in terms of righteous roles?

Gifts by Which to Remember the Savior

After studying the Savior's life there can be no doubt that the Father and Jesus Christ both love the women and the men, their brothers and sons, their sisters and daughters. Elder Bruce R. Mc-Conkie said, "It is wholesome and proper to look for similitudes of Christ everywhere and to use them repeatedly in keeping him and his laws uppermost in our minds" (*The Promised Messiah* [Salt Lake City: Deseret Book Company, 1978], p. 453). With this in mind we note that both God's sons and his daughters have been given special gifts to help them keep in remembrance the Savior and his laws. These gifts help them feel one with him, help them draw closer to him by reminding them of him daily.

For the worthy sons of God this gift is the holy priesthood. It is through righteous exercise of that priesthood that worthy men experience priesthood power as the Savior did. Several years ago I was in a committee meeting where the discussion turned to priesthood blessings. One of the men with tears in his eyes recounted a time when he had laid his hands on a child's head and in the course of the blessing felt the mighty power of the priesthood as if it were electricity flow through his arms and hands and into the child.

Later I asked my husband if he had ever had a similar experience. He told me that while it did not happen with every blessing, it was not uncommon to feel that power when giving a blessing or performing an ordinance. Even if a man never feels this power "like electricity," he has the authority of the priesthood, the authority to offer to others the ordinances of the priesthood just as Jesus Christ did.

This great gift given to worthy men serves as a constant reminder of the Savior. This gift helps focus a man's mind on Jesus Christ. In this way he experiences, on a smaller scale, things similar to those the Savior experienced. He is drawn closer to Jesus as he does the very things Jesus did. He is encouraged and helped to remember Jesus in a way that makes the Savior empirically real and brings him very near.

As men recognize the responsibility of the priesthood and honor it, they experience the power of that priesthood more and more. In ordinations, blessings, in any way the priesthood is exercised, they have the privilege, dependent upon their righteousness, to feel this empathy with the Savior.

Women have been given a much different gift, but it is similar in that it too can remind them of the Savior and what he did for mankind. Women sacrifice of their very life's blood for the possibility of giving physical life. This can be a reminder that the Savior sacrificed his blood for the possibility of spiritual life for all of God's children.

Every person on this earth is here because of the blood sacrifice of a mortal woman. Elder Bruce R. McConkie explains that "blood is an element that pertains exclusively to mortality" and that "blood became the life preserving element in the natural body" (*Mormon Doctrine*, 2nd ed. [Salt Lake City: Bookcraft, 1966], pp. 268, 269). A woman makes this sacrifice of the necessary "preserving element" in her own body in order to give another spirit a body and mortal life.

Likewise, spiritual life could not happen without the sacrifice of the Savior's blood. As he willingly sacrificed his essential "preserving element" he gave to all of us immortal life and the possibility of eternal salvation. This comparison is made in the Pearl of Great Price. "By reason of transgression cometh the fall, which fall bringeth death, and *inasmuch as ye were born into the world by water, and blood, and the spirit,* which I have made, and so became of dust a living soul, even so ye must be born again into the kingdom of heaven, of water, and of the Spirit, *and be cleansed by blood, even the blood of mine Only Begotten;* that ye might be sanctified from all sin, and enjoy the words of eternal life in this world, and eternal life in the world to come, even immortal glory" (Moses 6:59, italics added).

As a worthy daughter of God grows closer to her Heavenly Father, the symbolism takes on added meaning. The gift gives her a special empathy and feeling for the atonement the Savior made for us and an increased understanding of the law of sacrifice. Any woman who has borne a child knows that physical life does not come without pain and effort. Likewise spiritual life cannot occur without pain and effort. When we recognize these symbolisms it is not difficult to understand why the adversary has tried to make such wonderful gifts into embarrassments. Satan doesn't want a woman to feel closer to the Savior, so he demeans and debases the gift.

Besides the symbolism, the pain and suffering that women experience during pregnancy and childbirth tend to draw closer to the Savior those who are seeking him. Although their pain is not nearly as intense or all-encompassing as the Savior's suffering was, those moments of giving life are often moments of empathy and love for the Savior. They are sacred moments.

I have a dear friend who understood that childbearing is a sacred partnership with God and prayed during her third pregnancy that this birth would help her better understand the spiritual significance of childbearing. During the bearing down stage of labor the great exertion caused the capillaries in her skin to hemorrhage, causing pinpoint red marks to cover her face and neck, a condition known medically as *petechiae*. Although her bleeding was not through the pores as was the Savior's or her suffering as intense, her prayer was answered in a way she never expected. The life-giving aspects of the Atonement have become very real to her, and several months later she is still pondering and learning from that experience more about the similarities of physical and spiritual birth, about the Atonement, about what the Savior had to bear, and about his intense love for us.

These gifts given to women help sisters who so desire to share (on a smaller scale) with the Savior, and to draw closer to him in a way that through emotions and thoughts make him and what he has given mankind very real. These gifts remind women of the Savior. But why is it important that we be reminded and share with Jesus Christ in our daily lives? Because the most important task of this life is to become one with him, and daily reminders of him help us to do that. When we begin to remember him in all we do and think, then we also make "onement" with our spouse easier.

Imagine how formidable marriage would be if through trial and error we had to first define and then adapt and merge and combine with each other in order to be one. It would be like two people shooting at a very large target that had no markings and both trying to hit the same unmarked place at the same time. But if two people shoot at the same time at a target that has a well-defined bull's-eye, suddenly the task of hitting the same place becomes easier. We have been given a well-defined target, Jesus Christ. Our task as husbands and wives is simply to conform to him. What a hopeless situation it would be without him! How beautiful it is with him and how rich and rewarding is a marriage in which both partners are striving to be one with Christ!

Both men and women are strengthened as they follow the Savior's example, abandon the task of keeping self and others within male and female stereotypes, and instead help each other to attain righteousness. To do this we must better understand priesthood and what a help meet is. The real benefit of such an understanding, however, will come to succeeding generations who are raised by parents who have become one in Jesus Christ.

Therefore, blessed are ye if ye continue in my goodness, a light unto the Gentiles, and through this priesthood, a savior unto my people Israel. The Lord hath said it. Amen.

—D&C 86:11

CHAPTER 5

Stewards of the Life-Giving Ordinances

A teacher opened a Sunday School class with the question, "What is priesthood?" I was surprised at the variety of answers: "God's form of government." "The power to command in God's name." "The power to know God." "The authority of God."'

Priesthood Definition

None of the answers was wrong, but they were very different from each other and did not contain the total essence of priesthood. Each answer was instead a partial definition. Elder Bruce R. McConkie wrote: "As pertaining to eternity, priesthood is the eternal power and authority of Deity by which all things exist; by which they are created, governed, and controlled; by which the universe and worlds without number have come rolling into existence; by which the great plan of creation, redemption, and exaltation operates throughout immensity. It is the power of God." (*Mormon Doctrine*, 2nd ed. [Salt Lake City: Bookcraft, 1966], p. 594.)

The Prophet Joseph Smith explained "that the spirits of men are eternal, that they are governed by the same Priesthood that Abraham, Melchizedek, and the Apostles were: that they are organized according to that Priesthood which is everlasting, 'without beginning of days or end of years.' " (*Teachings of the Prophet Joseph Smith*, comp. Joseph Fielding Smith [Salt Lake City: Deseret Book Company, 1976], p. 208.)

In addition the Prophet Joseph Smith explained:

> The Melchizedek Priesthood comprehends the Aaronic or Levitical Priesthood . . . and is the channel through which all knowledge, doctrine, the plan of salvation and every important matter is revealed from heaven.
>
> Its institution was prior to "the foundation of this earth, or the morning stars sang together, or the Sons of God shouted for joy," and is the highest and holiest Priesthood, and is after the order of the Son of God, and all other Priesthoods are only parts, ramifications, powers and blessings belonging to the same, and are held, controlled, and directed by it. It is the channel through which the Almighty commenced revealing His glory at the beginning of the creation of this earth, and through which He has continued to reveal Himself to the children of men to the present time, and through which He will make known His purposes to the end of time. (*Teachings of the Prophet Joseph Smith*, pp. 166–67.)

From these statements we see that the priesthood is much more than we usually consider. Most of the blessings and gifts that God shares with man are by virtue of his priesthood power. These blessings and gifts are given to men, women, and children. Alma tells us, "And now [the Lord] imparteth his word by angels unto men, yea, not only men but women also. Now this is not all; little children do have words given unto them many times, which confound the wise and the learned" (Alma 32:23).

Heavenly Father gives all people born into the world the blessing of the light of Christ. In addition, he gives us individual talents and abilities. Those people who follow the light of Christ, who are baptized and receive the gift of the Holy Ghost, receive more blessings and gifts. Progression then continues under the influence of the Spirit until the person enters a temple of the Lord where he or she is further endowed. When one enters the holy state of matrimony in the temple one receives the blessing of entering an order of the priesthood. Finally, in the temple, the promises of the fullness of the priesthood can be obtained. In this manner, attaining through righteousness line upon line and precept upon precept, men and women can gain more and more of the blessings of the priesthood until they eventually become like God.

Brigham Young said: "There is no act of a Latter-day Saint— no duty required—no time given, exclusive and independent of the Priesthood. Everything is subject to it, whether preaching, business, or any other act pertaining to the proper conduct of this life." (*Journal of Discourses* 7:66.)

We are told in the scriptures that priesthood is divided into two parts, the lesser priesthood or Aaronic Priesthood being an appendage to the greater, or the Melchizedek Priesthood (see Doctrine and Covenants 107:14). The Aaronic Priesthood holds the keys to the ministering of angels (see D&C 107:20) and the Melchizedek Priesthood holds the keys to the knowledge of God (see D&C 84:19). "The power and authority of the higher, or Melchizedek Priesthood, is to hold the keys of all the spiritual blessings of the church—to have the privilege of receiving the mysteries of the kingdom of heaven, to have the heavens opened unto them, to commune with the general assembly and church of the Firstborn, and to enjoy the communion and presence of God the Father, and Jesus the mediator of the new covenant" (D&C 107:18-19).

Elder James E. Talmage explained: "In the restored Church of Jesus Christ, the Holy Priesthood is conferred, as an individual bestowal, upon men only, and this in accordance with Divine requirement. It is not given to woman to exercise the authority of the Priesthood independently; nevertheless, in the sacred endowments associated with the ordinances pertaining to the House of the Lord, woman shares with man the blessings of the Priesthood." ("The Eternity of Sex," *Young Woman's Journal* 25 [1914]: 602.)

Thus we see that priesthood in the eternal sense is the power of God and that the blessings of the priesthood are available to every worthy man or woman who seeks them. These powers and blessings encompass all that we are and have and do and all that we righteously hope for. As the Prophet Joseph said, the priesthood has "parts, ramifications, powers and blessings belonging to the same"; and "all Priesthood is Melchizedek, but there are different portions or degrees of it" (*Teachings of the Prophet Joseph Smith*, pp. 167, 180).

What we have been defining is priesthood in its broadest, grandest, eternal sense which includes the powers and blessings that come from priesthood. But for these powers and blessings to be shared, directed and actualized as they need to be, there must be some form of organization and government. To accomplish this ordering, worthy male members of the Church are ordained to and given offices and callings in the priesthood. The word *ordain* comes from the Latin word *ordinare* which means "to set in order." Everything in God's kingdom has an order and it is a primary function of priesthood to establish and maintain that order.

"As pertaining to man's existence on this earth, priesthood is the *power and authority* of God delegated to man on earth to act in all things for the salvation of men" (*Mormon Doctrine*, p. 594, italics added). This power and authority is delegated by God to men and gives them the right to govern the Church and to administer the life-giving ordinances of the gospel.

There are a few traditional "traps" that keep us from understanding priesthood as we should. One is the need to differentiate between priesthood and office in the priesthood. "Sometimes we hear brethren refer to 'magnifying the priesthood.' While many of us are guilty of making this erroneous statement, it isn't the priesthood we magnify; it is one's office and calling in the priesthood. It cannot be enlarged upon because there is no authority or power greater in the universe." (Delbert L. Stapley, in Conference Report, Mexico and Central America Area Conference, 1972, p. 64.)

The second trap Church members can fall into is using the terms *priesthood* and *men* as synonyms. They are not the same thing. We might hear an announcement that the priesthood has the assignment to clean the church grounds when we really mean that the priesthood *bearers* have the assignment. I once told some friends that my husband is very good at a certain sport. One man jokingly replied, "It's good to hear you women compliment the priesthood." But the compliment had nothing to do with priesthood.

It is dangerous for men or women to think that a man is the priesthood. He is not. He is a man who holds an office in the priesthood, but even that office is not, in and of itself, the priesthood. As Elder Bruce R. McConkie clarified: "The priesthood is greater than any of its offices. No office adds any power, dignity, or authority to the priesthood. All offices derive their rights, prerogatives, graces, and powers from the priesthood." (*Mormon Doctrine*, p. 595.)

Priesthood Callings and Service

This leads us to a vital question. Why does a man hold office in the priesthood? The answer is important: One of the most significant ways a man works out his salvation is by magnifying the priesthood office and calling he holds. Also, John Taylor said, "We are here as saviors of men" (*Journal of Discourses*, 26 vols. [Liverpool: F. D. Richards & Sons, 1855–86], 24:268).

A savior is someone who does something for others that they cannot do for themselves. A man holding the priesthood serves, sacrifices, and offers to others the saving ordinances of the priesthood which they cannot administer to themselves; he thus becomes a savior. This service is important to others and also to the priesthood bearer, for only by being a savior does he put himself in a position to be saved.

According to the great plan of salvation Adam and Eve fell which allowed them to procreate. But in addition to posterity the Fall brought death and sin into the world. Death and sin were barriers that would keep Adam and Eve and each of us from progressing and returning to the Eternal Father. Therefore, Jesus Christ came to earth and performed the Atonement, which overcame death and sin. The word *atonement* means "at onement," or the act of setting at one. In other words, the Atonement removed the barriers of death and sin which blocked man's path back to God; thus making it possible for mankind to be restored to the Father, to become one with him. Because Jesus was the one who overcame the obstacles, he is the Mediator. He is the one who can change us or reconcile us to the Father. Because of his perfect life he also became the model.

The purpose of men holding the priesthood is to assist the Savior in setting things at one or bringing about "at onement" by preventing spiritual death. The power over spiritual death or sin is found in the ordinances of the priesthood. The authority to administer these saving ordinances is obtained by being ordained to an office in the priesthood by one who already has that authority; there is no other way. This authority is a special gift which allows a man to serve, to be a savior to his fellowmen.

Elder Stephen L Richards said: "The Priesthood of God means to me only the right to serve, in the name of God, God's children, and he who serves God's children in God's name is doing the greatest service for the Master that can be done" (Conference Report, October 1917, p. 147). This same concept was discussed by the First Presidency in 1914:

> Priesthood is not given for the honor or aggrandizement of man, but for the ministry of service among those for whom the bearers of that sacred commission are called to labor. Be it remembered that even our Lord and Master, after long fasting, when faint in body and physically weakened by exhausting vigils and continued abstinence, resisted the arch tempter's suggestion that he use the authority and power of his Messiahship to provide for his own immediate needs.
>
> The God-given titles of honor and of more than human distinction associated with the several offices in and orders of the Holy Priesthood, are not to be used nor considered as are the titles originated by man; they are not for adornment nor are they expressive of mastership, but rather of appointment to humble service in the work of the one Master whom we profess to serve. (Joseph F. Smith, Anthon H. Lund, Charles W. Penrose, "On Titles," *Improvement Era*, March 1914, p. 479.)

The Doctrine and Covenants summarizes this with the powerful verse: "He that is ordained of God and sent forth, the same is appointed to be the greatest, notwithstanding he is the least and the servant of all" (D&C 50:26).

In all its majesty and splendor, priesthood is summarized best in terms of service. This service includes kindness, helping, giving offerings, and many things that all of God's children should be doing; it also means sharing the ordinances, a service that not everyone can do. These ordinances are the power to overcome spiritual death and are a sacred, important trust. Each of the saving ordinances a man performs allows those he serves to draw closer to their Savior and their Eternal Father. Baptism that washes away sin, the gift of the Holy Ghost that directs one away from sin and to God, the sacrament, which renews the baptismal covenant, and the ordinances of the temple—these are all meant to prevent spiritual death, thereby enabling us to have new life. Even the anointing of the sick can involve a remission of sins. James wrote: "Is any sick among you? let him call for the elders of the church; and let them pray over him, anointing him with oil in the name of the Lord: and the prayer of faith shall save the sick, and the Lord shall raise him up; and if he have committed sins, they shall be forgiven him" (James 5:14-15).

A man helps others become one with Jesus Christ by administering the ordinances of the priesthood; and in so serving he progresses toward godhood himself. In truth, godhood is service. God helps us, guides us, serves us. Our earthly sojourn is meant to be a practice for becoming gods or a practice in service. Without means and ways to serve we could not become like God. Serving in priesthood offices and callings is a special way God has provided for men to perform the works they need to accomplish in order to become gods. By serving and offering the ordinances a man cleanses himself of the sins of his generation. Thus priesthood service benefits the one serving as well as the one being served.

Priesthood Is Primarily for Families

We usually think of the government part of priesthood in terms of the adminstrative offices of the Church. Bishops, stake presidents, high councilors, quorum presidencies—all serve the Church and function in priesthood callings. This is a very important part of priesthood service, but when we analyze priesthood carefully it appears that it is designed to be primarily used for and in the family. Even when the priesthood functions outside the family, the reason is to strengthen individuals and families and to give to other people the ordinances and the power so that they in turn can share these great blessings with their families.

In the beginning priesthood was given to families, not wards or stakes. Adam was the first high priest, and all that existed at that time was his immediate family. He used his priesthood to serve his family through worship, teaching, and ministering. From Adam, priesthood was passed down to his righteous sons, who in turn ministered to their families. Abraham, Isaac, and Jacob all had the priesthood. As far as we know, they didn't administer wards or stakes; they ministered to wives and children.

Priesthood Through the Dispensations

After Moses delivered the children of Israel (after more than four hundred years they were still known as Israel's family) out of bondage the Melchizedek Priesthood was taken away from Israel generally, but the Aaronic Priesthood remained. Elder Bruce R. McConkie explained that the Lord "took the Melchizedek Priesthood, which administers the gospel, out of their midst in the sense that it did not continue and pass from one priesthood holder to another in the normal and usual sense of the word. The keys of the priesthood were taken away with Moses so that any future priesthood ordinations required special divine authorization." (*The Mortal Messiah*, 4 vols. [Salt Lake City: Deseret Book Company, 1979–81], 1:60.)

In the priesthood that remained, only the men of the family of Levi ministered in the priesthood. Thus even with this larger group, the priesthood was restricted to a family. It then became the privilege and responsibility of the tribe of Levi to minister to the extended family—the other tribes of Israel.

During the time between Moses and Christ, only the prophets possessed the right to the higher priesthood and thus to the blessings that could bring men into the presence of God. Joseph Smith explained, "All the prophets had the Melchizedek Priesthood and were ordained by God himself" (*Teachings of the Prophet Joseph Smith*, p. 181).

With the coming of the Savior a new dispensation began and the Melchizedek Priesthood was restored to the earth. On the Mount of Transfiguration the keys of the priesthood were given to Peter, James and John to carry on the priesthood in that dispensation. (See Luke 9:28–30; *Teachings of the Prophet Joseph Smith*, p. 158.) This made it possible for the Church to function with twelve apostles and seventies and officers and teachers who held and administered the priesthood. In a short time, however, apostasy destroyed the church and priesthood authority was again taken from the earth.

With the restoration of the gospel through Joseph Smith, the Lord once more restored the keys of the priesthood. The same organization that had been established at the time of the Savior was again set up. Worthy men could now be ordained to the priesthood in order to function in offices and callings of Church government and to serve their families. With this authority Joseph Smith was able to organize a Church whose purpose was to help in teaching and serving the family. The priesthood then became available to many families. Even then, however, there were restrictions as to which men could hold priesthood office. It was not until June 8, 1978, that all worthy men regardless of race could obtain this great gift. What a great blessing that is to the world!

But it is only a blessing if it is used properly. Said President Wilford Woodruff: "Let all Israel remember that the eternal and everlasting priesthood is bestowed upon us for the purpose alone of administering in the ordinances of life and salvation, both for the living and the dead, and no man on earth can use that priesthood for any other purpose than for the work of the ministry, the perfecting of the Saints, edifying the body of Christ, establishing the kingdom of heaven, and redeeming Zion. If we attempt to use it for unrighteous purposes, like lightning from heaven, our power, sooner or later, falls, and we fail to accomplish the designs of God." (Wilford Woodruff, *The Discourses of Wilford Woodruff*, sel. G. Homer Durham [Salt Lake City: Bookcraft, 1969], pp. 69–70.)

What a great day we live in! Every worthy male may now hold the priesthood, the Church is organized with Apostles and prophets, high priests, elders, priests, teachers, and deacons, yet the real purpose of priesthood has not changed. The priesthood still exists to bless families by enabling family members to become one with God. As Elder Bruce R. McConkie said, "The family is the most important organization in time or in eternity" ("Only An Elder," *Ensign,* June 1975, p. 67).

Priesthood, Families, and the Quest for Zion

As a worthy priesthood holder presides in a home, he strengthens his family through the authority of the priesthood. But the blessings come only as he exercises and uses his priesthood as a means to serve, to become a savior. One of the most important ways he does this is to use his priesthood to assist in the spiritual rebirth of his family. When authorized to do so he can baptize and confirm a person a member of the Church and bestow the gift of the Holy Ghost. He can bless and thereby empower. He can call his family together for prayer and fasting. He can teach. He can direct. He can influence. He can call upon God for direction and guidance and expect an answer. He can lead his family back to God. But most of all he can establish Zion within his own home. Joseph Smith answered the question, "What is meant by the command in Isaiah . . . 'Put on thy strength, O Zion?' " as follows: "[Isaiah] had reference to those whom God should call in the last days, who should hold the power of priesthood to bring again Zion, and the redemption of Israel; and to put on her strength is to put on the authority of the priesthood, which she, Zion, has a right to by lineage; also to return to that power which she had lost." (D&C 113:7-8.) And it is in families, within our homes, that Zion will be first established.

But as Elder H. Burke Peterson explained: "Some brethren do not understand that there is a marked difference between priesthood authority and priesthood power. The two terms are not necessarily synonymous. *Authority* in the priesthood comes by the laying on of hands by one having the proper authority. However, according to revelation from the Lord, *power* in the priesthood comes only through righteous living." ("Unrighteous Dominion," *Ensign*, July 1989, p. 9.) It is only through the righteous use of priesthood power and authority that Zion will be established. Zion is defined as "the pure in heart" (D&C 97:21). The pure in heart are those who have been cleansed and become one with God the Father and his Son Jesus Christ. This brings us back to the topic of "onement" and its importance. It is through the ordinances and powers of the priesthood that men and women can be one with God.

Balance and Interdependency

Even within the priesthood, we find the balance that gives the gospel its beauty. Even though a man may be worthy and hold the priesthood, he is just as dependent upon other priesthood holders as is a woman. He is also dependent upon women to provide the people to offer the ordinances to. As to his own salvation, a man must be baptized and confirmed and receive the temple ordinances; he must be sealed to a worthy woman by someone authorized to perform the sacred sealing ordinance. He can be helped in time of decision or sickness or emergency by receiving a priesthood blessing. He does none of this to or for himself!

Men who recognize this interdependency within the priesthood, who humble themselves and serve others through their priesthood, understand the authority they hold. These men know that priesthood holders are the stewards over the ordinances of the gospel and that it is through the ordinances that spiritual rebirth is made possible. But they also know that the power necessary for that rebirth is not self-contained; even more than they are dependent upon priesthood holders, men and women are dependent upon Jesus Christ.

Stewards of the Ordinances

The dictionary defines *steward* as one who is entrusted with the management of property, finances, or other affairs not his own. When a man functions in the priesthood he is a steward standing in place of Jesus Christ, whose property and affairs are being managed by authorized mortals. At the Last Supper and again when appearing to the Nephites after his resurrection, the Savior administered the sacrament himself. On those occasions he did not have Peter or Nephi bless the sacrament; he did it himself. When Jesus is not present, however, a worthy priesthood holder takes his place to say the words and do the things the Savior would do.

Priesthood holders are stewards over the ordinances that make possible spiritual life. In order to fulfill this stewardship priesthood holders must offer the gospel and its ordinances to the world. What a sacred responsibility! What an honor it is to be asked to share in the Savior's work and glory of "bring[ing] to pass the immortality and eternal life of man" (Moses 1:39). This is one of man's greatest endeavors: to serve by helping to give his brothers and sisters, his wife and children, power over spiritual death. It is a pursuit that prepares one for godhood and, in fact, is a practice in godhood. Joseph Smith explained: "Those holding the fulness of the Melchizedek Priesthood are kings and priests of the Most High God, holding the keys of power and blessings. In fact, that Priesthood is a perfect law of theocracy, and stands as God to give laws to the people, administering endless lives to the sons and daughters of Adam." (*Teachings of the Prophet Joseph Smith*, p. 322.)

"Only upon the Principles of Righteousness"

For priesthood to prevent spiritual death and empower others with spiritual rebirth it must operate through the principles of righteousness. Elder Hugh B. Brown said: "I should like to say to you fathers tonight that our conduct in our homes determines in large measure our worthiness to hold and exercise the priesthood, which is the power of God delegated to man. Almost any man can make a good showing when on parade before the public, but one's integrity is tested when 'off duty.' The real man is seen and known in the comparative solitude of the home. An office or title will not erase a fault nor guarantee a virtue." (Conference Report, April 1962, p. 88.)

The warning is also given in the Doctrine and Covenants:

> Behold, there are many called, but few are chosen. And why are they not chosen?
>
> Because their hearts are set so much upon the things of this world, and aspire to the honors of men, that they do not learn this one lesson —
>
> That the rights of the priesthood are inseparably connected with the powers of heaven, and that the powers of heaven cannot be controlled nor handled only upon the principles of righteousness.
>
> That they may be conferred upon us, it is true; but when we undertake to cover our sins, or to gratify our pride, our vain ambition, or to exercise control or dominion or compulsion upon the souls of the children of men, in any degree of unrighteousness, behold, the heavens withdraw themselves; the Spirit of the Lord is grieved; and when it is withdrawn, Amen to the priesthood or the authority of that man. (D&C 121:34–37.)

The warning in the beginning of this quotation should be stressed. Some men today have been ordained to the priesthood but are failing in their calling to be saviors of men because they have abdicated their role as stewards over the life-giving ordinances and are instead pursuing the pleasures and recognition of the world. Both of these problems are centered in selfishness. Selfishness is the greatest enemy to righteousness. Selfishness keeps both men and women from their duties and consequently from the peace and joy the gospel has to offer.

However, to those who choose to overcome the natural selfishness of man, who choose to accept the responsibility of their stewardship, power is given. President Spencer W. Kimball explained: "There is no limit to the power of the priesthood which you hold. The limit comes in you if you do not live in harmony with the Spirit of the Lord and you limit yourselves in the power you exert." (*The Teachings of Spencer W. Kimball*, ed. Edward L. Kimball [Salt Lake City: Bookcraft, 1982], p. 498.)

To fully understand this quotation we need to understand that priesthood is the power to accomplish God's purposes. A man cannot use his priesthood to do whatever he wants; he can use his priesthood only to do what God wants. Therefore, before a man can use the power or authority of the priesthood he must through revelation and inspiration come to know the will of God. The will of God, his plans and purposes, cannot be frustrated. "Remember, remember that it is not the work of God that is frustrated, but the work of men" (D&C 3:3). The authority of God is given to man to accomplish his purposes. Knowledge is power, but more specifically, the knowledge of God's will is power.

In the Doctrine and Covenants the warning is given: "For although a man may have many revelations, and have power to do many mighty works, yet if he boasts in his own strength, and sets at naught the counsels of God, and follows after the dictates of his own will and carnal desires, he must fall and incur the vengeance of a just God upon him" (D&C 3:4). Even when a man uses priesthood power to accomplish a mighty work, it is not the man that is doing it. At all times he must realize that the work was performed because of the power of God, because it was God's will, but not because of himself. He was an instrument.

Priesthood entitles a man, if called, to preside in the Church. Not every man will have that opportunity. But every husband is entitled to preside in his home, and through the authority of his priesthood to establish Zion in his family. The power to establish Zion, however, comes only through righteous living. Many men have the authority but lack the power to bring Zion about. Said President Lorenzo Snow: "We have the same Priesthood that Jesus had, and we have got to do as He did, to make sacrifice of our own desires and feelings as He did, perhaps not to die martyrs as He did, but we have got to make sacrifices in order to carry out the purposes of God, or we shall not be worthy of this holy Priesthood, and be saviors of the world" (*Journal of Discourses* 23:341–42).

On the matter of obtaining the fulness of the priesthood, President Joseph Fielding Smith explained: "Joseph Smith said: 'If a man get a fulness of the priesthood of God, he has to get it in the same way that Jesus Christ obtained it, and that was by keeping all the commandments and obeying all the ordinances of the house of the Lord.' I hope we understand that. If we want to receive the fulness of the priesthood of God, then we must receive the fulness of the ordinances of the house of the Lord and keep his commandments. . . . No man can get the fulness of the priesthood outside of the temple of the Lord." (*Doctrines of Salvation*, comp. Bruce R. McConkie, 3 vols. [Salt Lake City: Bookcraft, 1954–56], 3:131.)

A man serves as a patriarch in the home. It is his right to officiate in righteousness, but as President Spencer W. Kimball said: "No woman has ever been asked by the Church authorities to follow her husband into an evil pit. She is to follow him as he follows and obeys the Savior of the world, but in deciding this, she should always be sure she is fair." ("The Blessings and Responsibilities of Womanhood," in *Woman* [Salt Lake City: Deseret Book Company, 1979], p. 83.) This law of obedience puts a tremendous responsibility upon the husband's shoulders. The adverb *as* means "to the same degree or in the same manner that." So the wife obeys the husband in the same manner or the same degree that he obeys the Savior. Thus the man is given the right to preside, but the woman is given the responsibility to judge how he presides.

I learned a similar principle when my children began to grow. If I allowed one child to cut a cake or pie for the others, the best way to ensure justice was to allow the ones who didn't cut to have the first choices as to which pieces they got.

We see this balance of "presider" and "judge" exemplified in the story of Abraham and again in the life of Jacob. Abraham was entering Egypt when the Lord told him that the Egyptians would desire his wife Sarah and would kill him so that she would then be a widow and the pharaoh would be free to marry her. The Lord, therefore, instructed Abraham to ask Sarah to tell the Egyptians that she was Abraham's sister. Abraham's life was now in Sarah's hands and her answer became her judgment on Abraham, for she was to obey him *as* he had obeyed the Lord.

If Abraham had not cared for Sarah as the Savior does his people, if he had not obeyed the Lord in fulfilling his responsibility to her and to the Lord, she might have obeyed as he had obeyed—

which might have been not at all—and the Egyptians would have killed him. But Abraham had obeyed the Lord, so Sarah obeyed as he had; and by her so doing Abraham's life was spared.

Abraham explains it this way: "And it came to pass that I, Abraham, told Sarai, my wife, all that the Lord had said unto me—Therefore say unto them, I pray thee, thou art my sister, that it may be well with me for thy sake, and *my soul shall live because of thee*" (Abraham 2:25, italics added).

As a wife gives herself to her husband and he receives her she is a gift to him, and the responsibility for the welfare and care of the gift falls to the receiver. It stands to reason that at some point an accounting must be made as to how the gift was cared for. Thus the eternal destiny of every man's soul, as was Abraham's, will in part be determined by how he treated his wife.

Righteous Women Assist

In the scriptures there is a theme of righteous women, in their role as helps meet, being called upon to assist the work of the priesthood in giving spiritual life. Moses owes his life to four women. First is the obvious gift of life from his mother, Jochebed. Shortly after birth his life was preserved by his sister, Miriam, as she tended him in the bulrushes. Next Pharaoh's daughter literally saved him from the sword of Pharaoh. And finally his wife Zipporah preserved his life when he had sinned. Of this story the Joseph Smith Translation of the Bible says: "The Lord was angry with Moses, and his hand was about to fall upon him, to kill him; for he had not circumcised his son. Then Zipporah took a sharp stone and circumcised her son, and cast the stone at his feet, and said, Surely thou art a bloody husband unto me. And the Lord spared Moses and let him go, because Zipporah, his wife, circumcised the child. And she said, Thou art a bloody husband. And Moses was ashamed, and hid his face from the Lord, and said, I have sinned before the Lord." (JST, Exodus 4:24–26.)

Blood is a symbol of our mortal state and of the guilt that comes from disobedience (spiritual death). What Zipporah apparently means by "Thou art a bloody husband" is that Moses was guilty of disobedience and was partaking of spiritual death instead of spiritual life. Zipporah saved Moses from physical and spiritual death by performing the circumcision that he for some reason did not do. If even the prophets have needed the assistance and strengths of a righteous wife, how much more does a man of this day need the help of a righteous wife to assist him through life's journey!

A friend once told me that when his family was in a hurry to eat he often forgot to call on someone to pray, so his wife would do it. This made him angry. Then one day he realized that instead of getting angry at her he should thank her. Yes, it would have been better if she had simply reminded him of his duty instead of doing it herself, but he realized that her intentions were good. He also realized that if he didn't perform his duties he would be held accountable, so when she called on someone to pray she was actually saving him from the consequences of forgetting the prayer. These realizations not only dissolved his feelings of anger but also helped him to be more diligent in his responsibilities.

The True Head

When a husband realizes how priesthood works and the role a help meet is to play in his life, when he seeks for order not through coercion but through righteousness, the whole family is blessed. When he exercises his right correctly, he also realizes that in a true patriarchal order God the Father and Jesus Christ are the heads of the home.

Carl and I have ten children—all of them daughters except the tenth. When our son was three I stopped before putting him down for a nap and asked who was in the picture on the wall. "Jesus," Joshua answered.

"And who is Jesus?" I asked.

"I don't know."

"He is our brother," I explained.

Joshua bristled and indignantly replied, "No, I am the brother!"

Some men carelessly fall into a trap of thinking they are the head in the sense of the ultimate head. But when a husband understands clearly that he is the patriarch under the direction of the Lord, he sees himself as the earthly administrator of a very sacred trust and his whole family is blessed. If he presides at all times by trying to ascertain and carry out the desires of his Heavenly Father and Jesus Christ, righteousness reigns in the home. When righteousness reigns, innumerable blessings follow.

One of the most significant blessings for the children raised in a righteous home is that the loving earthly patriarch becomes a model of the loving Heavenly Patriarch. In this way a father actually becomes a bridge between his children and their Heavenly Father. An all powerful, ever-loving, all-knowing Heavenly Father is easier to comprehend when an earthly father is earnestly striving toward righteousness.

As a father administers the ordinances of the priesthood, gives his children special father's blessings, and prays over and for his children morning and night, bonds are established that will last through all eternity; love is allowed to transfer from a dormant feeling to an empowering emotion; the Spirit abides in the home, and all who dwell there are enriched.

How can we thank our Father in Heaven enough for such a gift as priesthood? What power and strength a worthy man brings to a marriage and can give to posterity in this age of chaos and evil! What a wonderful gift—to have the authority to offer those you love the ordinances of spiritual rebirth that will allow them to become one with God!

It is not the power itself, however, but the offering of it to serve his family and God's family that helps the priesthood holder work out his own salvation. Fatherhood and priesthood are the most important stewardships a man can have. Magnifying his priesthood calling by sharing the life-giving ordinances is an important way for a man to obtain the faith, the gifts, the power that he needs to become like God. As a man comes to understand this and to serve well, he also establishes his part of the Eden relationship that is essential for a celestial marriage.

Favour is deceitful, and beauty is vain: but a woman that feareth the Lord, she shall be praised. Give her of the fruit of her hands; and let her own works praise her in the gates.

—Proverbs 31:30–31

CHAPTER 6

Stewards
of Life

*W*hen I first began to seriously search for answers concerning the woman's role, I received an impression to "study priesthood." This impression puzzled me. "I want to know about womanhood, not priesthood," I argued. But I set aside this first reaction and began to study priesthood. As I studied I was amazed at what I discovered. There is really no way to segregate the roles of man and woman. The two are so intertwined and so dependent upon each other, so balanced, that no woman and no man can understand his or her own role without also understanding the role of the other.

Marvelous Blessings
Available to Women

We discussed in the previous chapter how priesthood power and authority is conferred upon worthy men, but that both righteous men and righteous women of the Church are entitled to all the blessings of the priesthood as they seek to do their part in accomplishing God's purposes. Elder Bruce R. McConkie said:

"There are many marvelous powers and blessings which come to women in the Church and kingdom of God on earth which are not found anywhere else. The Lord has given us many things which bless and ennoble and exalt women beyond anything ever dreamed of outside his Church." (In Conference Report, Sydney Australia Area Conference 1976, p. 33.)

Elder McConkie further explained: "Women do not have the priesthood conferred upon them and are not ordained to offices therein, but they are entitled to all priesthood blessings. Those women who go on to their exaltation, ruling and reigning with husbands who are kings and priests, will themselves be *queens* and *priestesses*. They will hold positions of power, authority, and preferment in eternity." (*Mormon Doctrine*, 2nd ed. [Salt Lake City: Bookcraft, 1966], p. 594.)

The powers and blessings referred to are given to us if we seek them in righteousness. As we grow and progress, receive the Holy Ghost, and are endowed, we receive more and more enabling power and more spiritual gifts and blessings. When a couple is married for time and all eternity the husband and the wife enter into the patriarchal order of the priesthood. Simple logic tells us that fatherhood is part of that priesthood because God, from whom priesthood comes, chooses to be known by the title Father. A woman should realize that "motherhood is an eternal part of Priesthood" (John A. Widtsoe, *Evidences and Reconciliations* [Salt Lake City: Bookcraft, 1960], p. 308).

Many priesthood blessings such as the gift of the Holy Ghost are obvious and often discussed. Others are not so common and vary from person to person. David Whitmer tells of how his mother, Mary Musselman Whitmer, was given a special, unusual blessing. One night while on her way to milk the cow, she was met by a messenger who said, "You have been very faithful and diligent in your labors, but you are tired because of the increase of your toil; it is proper therefore that you should receive a witness that your faith may be strengthened." The messenger then untied his knapsack, removed the plates, and showed them to her, the same plates that Moroni had given Joseph Smith. As he turned the gold pages, he pointed out the characters engraved upon them and encouraged Mary to endure in faith. (See *Millennial Star* 40:773 and *Latter-day Saint Biographical Encyclopedia* 1:283.) Church history is full of accounts of righteous women who because of their faith were privileged with blessings and experiences of this caliber.

The Patriarchal Order

In an article entitled "What I Hope You Will Teach Your Children about the Temple," President Ezra Taft Benson said:

Adam and his posterity were commanded by God to be baptized, to receive the Holy Ghost, and to enter into the order of the Son of God.

To enter into the order of the Son of God is the equivalent today of entering into the fullness of the Melchizedek Priesthood, which is only received in the house of the Lord.

Because Adam and Eve had complied with these requirements, God said to them, "Thou art after the order of him who was without beginning of days or end of years, from all eternity to all eternity" (Moses 6:67) . . . .

The order of priesthood spoken of in the scriptures is sometimes referred to as the patriarchal order because it came down from father to son.

But this order is otherwise described in modern revelation as an order of family government where a man and woman enter into a covenant with God—just as did Adam and Eve—to be sealed for eternity, to have posterity, and to do the will and work of God throughout their mortality. . . .

Our Father's house is a house of order. We go to *His* house to enter into that order of priesthood which will entitle us to all that the Father hath, if we are faithful. For as the Lord has revealed in modern times, Abraham's seed are "lawful heirs" to the priesthood. (*Ensign*, August 1985, pp. 8—9, 10.)

When a man and woman enter into the patriarchal order of the priesthood they make promises and receive power and blessings that will help them return to God if they will but abide by those promises.

Women Help in Work of Priesthood

The very first expression of a woman's role was that she was to be a help meet. Before Eve was called woman, or mother of all living, she was called help meet. And what is a help meet to do? To assist in the work of the priesthood in whatever way the Lord commands. Just as a righteous man sees himself as servant to the Lord, a righteous woman sees herself as a handmaiden to the Lord. A woman whether married or not is an appropriate help in the work of the priesthood. She serves in stakes, wards, branches, and mission fields, teaching, leading, and ministering to her brothers and sisters. Her primary stewardship, however, is in the home—just as a man's is.

In the early days of the Restoration the Church was organized line upon line, precept upon precept. Presidencies, bishoprics, seventies, high councils, and missionaries were called and organized as the Lord instructed. In the spring of 1842 Eliza R. Snow was asked by a group of sisters to draw up a constitution and by-laws for a women's organization. She did so and presented them to Joseph Smith. He responded that they were the best he had ever seen. "But," he said, "this is not what you want. Tell the sisters their offering is accepted of the Lord, and He has something better for them than a written constitution. Invite them all to meet me and a few of the brethren in the Masonic Hall over my store next Thursday afternoon, and I will organize the sisters under the priesthood after a pattern of the priesthood." He further said, "The Church was never perfectly organized until the women were thus organized." ("Story of the Organization of the Relief Society," *The Relief Society Magazine* 6 [March 1919]: 129.)

Just as man was not complete alone, the Church itself was not complete, not "perfectly organized" until the women were organized into what we now call the Relief Society. This understanding helps us more fully comprehend the importance of helps meet in the kingdom of God. Helps meet are needed to do the work of the Lord in the home and in the Church.

This understanding also brings us to the realization that there is an area where the stewardships of men and women overlap. Both should be teaching, exhorting, and helping one another temporally and spiritually. However, there are specific gifts and responsibilities given to a woman to work out her salvation that are different from a man's.

Women Control Physical and Spiritual Life

As we discussed in chapter 5, a man holding the priesthood has the authority to administer the ordinances which are the power over spiritual death. In this way he is a savior to others. The appointed way of a help meet to be a savior, to work out her salvation, is to give life. This means procreating physical life if she can, but it includes much more than that. Women are to create life in the eternal sense of the word—physical and spiritual life. If we were to diagram the relationship of man's and woman's stewardships it would look something like this:

MAN'S STEWARDSHIP   WOMAN'S STEWARDSHIP

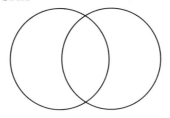

The scriptures provide examples of women who are saviors, who do for others what they cannot do for themselves. These examples show women giving spiritual and physical life, both literally and symbolically.

Esther saved the lives of all the Jews in Persia and Media. Even minor characters such as Shiphrah and Puah, two Hebrew midwives, spared the lives of many male babies though Pharaoh demanded that they be killed at birth (see Exodus 1:15-17). The prophetess Huldah, who was contemporary with the prophets Jeremiah and Zephaniah, gave spiritual life by prophesying of King Josiah's life and reign. Eve, Rebekah, Deborah, Elisabeth, and Mary all gave spiritual life as well as physical life by fulfilling their duties as helps meet.

There are only three Book of Mormon women mentioned by name. Two of the three are righteous and one of those two exemplifies this concept. Abish, a Lamanite woman converted to the gospel by a vision her father had, is present when Ammon, King Lamoni, and his wife, the queen are overcome by the Spirit and fall to the ground. Abish understands that this is the power of God and invites others to come and see what has happened, but the others do not believe her. Finally, Abish takes the queen by the hand and raises her up. Full of joy and love, the queen testifies of Jesus Christ and then takes her husband's hand and raises him up.

Each of these women accomplished her task in exactly the same way a man does: by listening and doing what the Spirit directed her to do. The reception and use of such blessings is always determined by righteousness.

Women and Doctrine and Covenants 25

In modern revelation the Lord has given women instructions as to how to be good helps meet. Section 25 begins by addressing Emma Smith, but it contains significant advice and promises for all women. Of this section President Gordon B. Hinckley said in the 1984 General Women's Meeting: "This is the only revelation given specifically to a woman, and in concluding it the Lord said, 'This is my voice unto all' (verse 16). Therefore, the counsel given by the Lord on this occasion is applicable to each of you." ("If Thou Art Faithful," *Ensign*, November 1984, p. 90.) In light of that, let's examine section 25 more closely.

Verse 2 reads, "A revelation I give unto you concerning my will; and if thou art faithful and walk in the paths of virtue before me, I will preserve thy life, and thou shalt receive an inheritance in Zion." It is often taught that if a woman is righteous she will share in the inheritance of her husband. When we understand "one-ment" we know that must be true. However, it seems to me that this verse also indicates that because of their own righteousness faithful women will receive an inheritance in which their husbands will share.

Next the Lord tells Emma, "thy sins are forgiven thee, and thou art an elect lady, whom I have called" (D&C 25:3). The Prophet Joseph Smith explained that elect means "to be elected to a certain work" (*History of the Church* 4:552). President Ezra Taft Benson in speaking to the sisters of the Church said, "I call you 'elect women,' for you have been elected by God to perform a unique and sacred work in our Heavenly Father's eternal plan" ("To the Elect Women of the Kingdom of God," in *Woman* [Salt Lake City: Deseret Book Company, 1979], p. 69).

Verse 4 warns, "Murmur not because of the things which thou hast not seen, for they are withheld from thee and from the world, which is wisdom in me in a time to come." This was directed to

Emma because of her discontent at not being able to see the plates, but it has as much meaning for sisters today. Perhaps this could also be an answer to the questions, "Why don't we know more about our Heavenly Mother?" and "Why don't we know more about the eternal destiny of women?" The advice in verse 4 is timely for those whose testimonies teeter because of what they do not know. Perhaps when our study has exhausted what we do have, or as we pray for answers, we will be given more. We must also consider President Joseph Fielding Smith's words, in which he declared, "The Lord is withholding knowledge from us because of our unworthiness" (*Doctrines of Salvation*, 3 vols., comp. Bruce R. McConkie [Salt Lake City: Bookcraft, 1972], 2:304). Perhaps as we righteously fulfill the duties we have already been given, we will be given more knowledge. Our present task is to continue in patience and faith, repentance and prayer, realizing that what we don't know in no way alters the truthfulness of what we do know and that the things withheld are kept from us in the wisdom of God.

Verse 5 explains that women are to be a comfort to their husbands and that consoling words and a spirit of meekness are the ways to be a comforter. In addition to being a comfort, such behavior encourages a man in the path of righteousness and willingness to lead and direct the family.

But what of those who have never married or are divorced or widowed? A righteous woman, whether married or not, should be preparing and practicing the use of consoling words and meekness so that when the time comes, whether in this life or the next, she is ready.

I have a friend in Mexico City with whom I correspond. After serving a mission, in her late twenties she married. In a letter she sent after the birth of her first child she explained how thrilled she was that wifehood and motherhood had finally come to her, and then she wrote: "Ever since I joined the Church I have prayed for the man I would someday marry. I did not know who that man would be, but my Heavenly Father did. I prayed that my Heavenly Father would protect my future husband and strengthen him and bless him with faith wherever he was and in whatever he was doing. Heavenly Father answered my prayer."

What a beautiful concept! Any worthy woman can comfort and console and pray for her true counterpart even if, at that moment, she does not know who he is!

But we limit ourselves if we confine our thoughts to mortality. Elder Parley P. Pratt wrote about the possibility of a person's dying early whom another person could or would otherwise have married:

> We may, perhaps, have had a friend of the other sex, whose pulse beat in unison with our own; whose every thought was big with aspirations, the hopes of a bright future in union with our own; whose happiness in time or in eternity would never be fully consummated without that union. Such a one, snatched from time in the very bloom of youth, lives in the other sphere with the same bright hope, watching our every footstep, in our meanderings through the rugged path of life, with longing desires for our eternal happiness and eager for our safe arrival in the same sphere. (*Key to the Science of Theology*, 9th ed. [Salt Lake City: Deseret Book Company, 1975], p. 76.)

Verse 7 of D&C 25 explains that women should expound scripture and exhort the Church as the Spirit directs. *Expound* means to define, to set forth in detail, to explain the meaning of. *Exhort* means to admonish, to persuade, to urge by earnest appeal. Both words imply a deep commitment and preparation. A woman cannot define in detail or explain the meaning of something she does not know well. Likewise it becomes difficult to persuade others to do something if one is not first doing that thing herself, especially in the home, where our actions are so closely observed. Fathers and mothers both share the responsibility to teach in the home; it is a primary responsibility. But this verse makes it clear that women are also to teach in the Church and to be an influence for good wherever the Spirit directs them to serve.

Verse 8 continues with the advice that time should be given to writing and to learning much. Writing is a wonderful way to sort out our thoughts. Keeping journals and attempting to explain thoughts and feelings while studying allows a person to organize and explore those thoughts in a deeper and more significant way. Spelling, punctuation, grammar—none of these matters unless you are writing for someone else. There is simply something about forcing feelings into words that makes them more our own and enhances the learning process.

Verse 9 instructs that a husband should also support his wife. In recent years it has been interesting to see in one case a mission president released so that his wife could serve as a general president in an auxiliary, and in another case a woman released as a general president and her husband called as a mission president. Is one spouse's calling more important than the other's? No! The time, the place, the purposes of the Lord—these are the things that matter. Only the Spirit can tell us which and whose duties are to take precedence when conflicts arise. Whatever the callings are, both spouses are doing the work of the Lord.

President Benson said: "Mother was Relief Society president in her ward, a small but solid country ward. I remember how important father considered her work in that assignment." ("To the Elect Women of the Kingdom of God," in *Woman*, p. 74.) The way a husband and wife support each other in their callings is very important in teaching their children respect and encouraging their testimony.

Verse 10 adds the always timely advice that we should lay aside the things of this world and seek for the things of a better. There is a joke that "a woman's place is in the mall." Sometimes it is too true to be a joke! There are many worldly things that sidetrack a woman from the things of a better world. Some women must beware of the "Martha syndrome"; a clean house is important since the Spirit cannot dwell in an unclean place, but struggling to keep a house totally sterile uses up time that could be spent in study, service, or other pursuits necessary for spiritual growth. Every human soul is at some time tempted with "the things of this world." It is important to recognize what our own challenges are and then overcome them.

Emma was next instructed to make a selection of hymns; verse 12 elaborates on what all women can learn from this: women can nurture through music. "For my soul delighteth in the song of the heart; yea, the song of the righteous is a prayer unto me, and it shall be answered with a blessing upon their heads" (D&C 25:12). Even those who do not perform on instruments or sing can provide wholesome music in their homes and in their teaching and training.

The next verses advise women to cleave unto the covenants, to continue in the spirit of meekness while guarding against pride, to delight in their husbands, and to keep the commandments continually. The section closes with the beautiful promise that if these things are done, a woman will receive a crown of righteousness.

Many women have wondered why this revelation doesn't talk about motherhood, but at the time it was given to Emma, in 1830, she and Joseph had been married for three years and had had only one child, who died within a few hours of birth. We don't know why Emma is not given advice for her future children, but the fact that motherhood isn't mentioned seems to indicate that the section is dealing with the role of Emma (and all women) as a help meet. When we consider that some women are never mothers and those who are spend only a portion of their lives raising children, we realize the importance of preparing and striving to be good helps meet — all women are called to be helps meet for their entire lives.

In speaking to a seminar held for Regional Representatives, President Gordon B. Hinckley said, "There are tremendous responsibilities for women in the Church as well as in the community consistent with and in total harmony with marriage, motherhood, and the rearing of good and able children." He also said, "Every young woman ought to be encouraged to refine her skills and increase her abilities, to broaden her knowledge and strengthen her capacity." (As quoted in *Ensign*, May 1988, p. 92.)

Equivalency in Primary Stewardships

A friend once complained that men are always one up on women. "Womanhood has manhood," she said, "sisterhood has brotherhood. There is servant and handmaiden, fatherhood and motherhood, but then men have priesthood." But priesthood does have an equivalent for women: help meet. What has confused us is that in the team of fatherhood and motherhood, mothers carry the greater responsibility of giving life while fathers assist, and in the team of priesthood and help meet priesthood carries the greater responsibility of preventing spiritual death while helps meet assist. Motherhood is the uniquely female way a woman serves, and priesthood is the uniquely male way a man serves; therefore, we often hear priesthood and motherhood equated.

Once more we see the equivalency, the balance, the partnership. The two work in a tandem relationship to help the family. A help meet does not hold priesthood, but she assists in the work of the priesthood. A father does not bear children, but he assists in the work of parenting. Each is dependent upon the other.

We find these primary stewardships symbolically represented in the scriptures by the women veiling their faces as Rebekah did upon seeing Isaac for the first time (see Genesis 24:65). Some biblical scholars have interpreted the veiling to be symbolic of a woman's submission to man, but her submission is not a submission of station or caste but to line of authority. Thus veiling does not symbolize it well. Besides this, headgear, such as a crown, is usually a symbol of power. In facsimile number 3 in the Pearl of Great Price in the explanation of figure 1 we read, "Abraham sitting upon Pharaoh's throne, by the politeness of the king, with a crown upon his head, representing the Priesthood." Abraham's headgear symbolizes the priesthood power he holds; it would seem reasonable, then, that a woman's headgear may be said to represent the power women hold—the power to procreate. The veil aptly portrays the internal nature of that power. Thus when Rebekah sees Isaac for the first time she veils her face—a symbol that she has come to add to his power of authority the power of creation. The union of the two powers, the external priesthood power of authority and the internal power of creation, makes a unit that is complete and whole.

Paul refers to this when he says, "For the man is not of the woman; but the woman of the man. Neither was the man created for the woman; but the woman for the man. For this cause ought the woman to have power on her head because of the angels." (1 Corinthians 11:8-10.) In the Joseph Smith Translation the word *power* has been changed to read, "a covering on her head." The woman was created to add to the man what he was lacking, the power to create life; and because this is her stewardship she covers or veils herself in symbolism of the power that is hers.

The next two verses in 1 Corinthians make more sense when we understand the symbolism of covering or veiling. "Nevertheless neither is the man without the woman, neither the woman without the man, in the Lord. [Both powers are necessary!] For as the woman is of the man, even so is the man also by the woman; but all things of God." (1 Corinthians 11:11-12.)

How grateful we should be for these ways to learn, to serve, to sacrifice; for sacrifice is essential for spiritual growth and eternal life. For women the most important sacrifice is to offer spiritual and physical life.

Motherhood and Maternity

The word *offering*, especially when applied to the physical, is important here. Too many people confuse the words *motherhood* and *maternity*. Not every woman who achieves the state of maternity is really a mother, while there are many women who never experience maternity but who mother by nurturing and offering life.

To explain further let us look more closely at the terms *mother* and *maternity*. *Maternity* is defined as "the state or condition of being a mother." But in addition to this physical relationship the term *mother* includes the definition, "anything that creates, nurtures, or protects something else." Those words—*create, nurture* and *protect*—become keys to a woman's understanding of her stewardship. While giving birth is one of the greatest ways a woman can be a savior, if the gift of physical life is not accompanied by love, by the nurturing of the spirit as well as the body, the woman is not truly a mother.

It is wrong to define womanhood in terms of maternity. The number of children or one's marital status are not the standards by which the Lord will judge a woman. She will be judged according to her desire and her opportunity. A woman with fifteen children who does not create bonds of love, who does not nurture or protect those children, is not truly a mother. A woman who cannot bear children, but who creates bonds of love and nurtures and protects wherever she can, is and will be an eternal mother.

Women: Breath of *Lives*

The Prophet Joseph Smith explained: "The 7th verse of 2nd chapter of Genesis ought to read—God breathed into Adam his spirit [i.e. Adam's spirit] or breath of life; but when the word 'ruach' applies to Eve, it should be translated lives." (*Teachings of the Prophet Joseph Smith,* comp. Joseph Fielding Smith [Salt Lake City: Deseret Book Company, 1976], p. 301.) In Hebrew the word *ruach* does not appear in the verse cited, so the Prophet is not trying to translate for us. Instead he is trying to teach us an important concept. The Hebrew word *ruach* (sometimes rendered *ruwach* in English) means "breath" or "by resemblance spirit." So God breathed into Adam his spirit or breath of life, but the Prophet appears to be explaining that what God gave Eve was the breath of not one life but of many lives.

Physically every female infant is born containing all the ova she will ever have, but the amount is staggering. At birth a female child will have one to two million egg cells in her ovaries. Thus a woman is born with the first cell of other lives, her children, tucked within her. The male body is different. It is born with the cells that will someday produce sperm, but the sperm are not produced until puberty. From puberty the male manufactures sperm, but it is not inherent in the body in the way ova are. This information helps us understand the quotation from Joseph Smith. A woman is not just life, she is lives. When you look at a newborn female child you are not looking at a life, but at the theoretical possibility of one to two million lives!

We are told in the scriptures that physical and spiritual creations mirror each other—"that which is spiritual being in the likeness of that which is temporal; and that which is temporal in the likeness of that which is spiritual; the spirit of man in the likeness of his person" (D&C 77:2). In the quotation cited Joseph Smith said that Eve's spirit is the breath of lives, so perhaps the female spirit contains the potential beginnings of other lives just as the female body does. This is only speculation; but we do know that mortal woman has within her not just her own being but also the first cell of many other lives—lives that are brought about by the assistance of the male.

If a woman is married and physically able to bear and rear children, her highest calling is to create, nurture, and protect those children. Throughout the Bible we see how important women felt their life-giving stewardship to be. Many of these women, however, found themselves barren. Women such as Rebekah, Sarah, Rachel, Elisabeth, and Hannah prayed and received miracles.

Rebekah's Example

One of the most interesting of these stories is that of Rebekah. Elder Bruce R. McConkie said, "I look upon Rebekah as one of the strongest characters mentioned in the whole body of revealed writ" (in *Studies in Scripture, Vol. 3: The Old Testament, Genesis to 2 Kings* [Sandy, Utah: Randall Book, 1985], p. 58). As such, Rebekah can tell us a lot about what the Lord expects of a righteous woman.

The scriptures don't tell us how old Rebekah was when she first enters the biblical narrative in Genesis 24 (the book of Jasher says she was ten years old). Abraham's eldest servant, Eliezer, (the name means God [*Eli*] is help [*ezer*]), had been sent from Canaan to Haran to find a wife for Isaac, who was forty years old. When Eliezer reached Haran he prayed for a sign that he would know the damsel who was to be Isaac's wife by the answer she would give to his request, "Let down thy pitcher, I pray thee, that I may drink."

Eliezer was not asking for a small sign! He had ten camels with him and had just made a journey of approximately 450 miles, which would take somewhere between eighteen and twenty days; and a single thirsty camel can drink up to twenty-six gallons of water in ten minutes! Eliezer is asking for a girl to answer his request for a drink with the reply, "Drink, and I will give thy [ten] camels drink also."

We are told that Rebekah was the first person Eliezer saw after he prayed. He watched her go down to the well and come back up. He then asked her for a drink, to which she replied: "Drink, my lord: and she hasted, and let down her pitcher upon her hand, and gave him drink. And when she had done giving him drink, she said, I will draw water for thy camels also, until they have done drinking." (Genesis 24:18–19.)

Rebekah must have been a selfless person and in tune with the Spirit in order to reply exactly as Eliezer had asked. After the camels were watered, Eliezer met Rebekah's family, arranged the marriage, and wanted to be on his way the very next morning. Rebekah's mother pleaded for him to wait at least ten days, but Eliezer insisted. "And they said, We will call the damsel, and enquire at her mouth. And they called Rebekah, and said unto her, Wilt thou go with this man? And she said, I will go." (Genesis 24:57–58.) Again we see the great faith Rebekah had. It is difficult to conceive of any motivation short of faith and trust in the Lord strong enough to cause a young girl to go with a strange man into a foreign land to marry a man she had never met. Apparently she knew this was what the Lord wanted her to do and was anxious to comply with his will.

The next morning as Rebekah was about to leave, she was given a blessing. Her parents and her brother knew that they would probably never see Rebekah again. What parting words, what most important blessing could they give her? "Thou art our sister, be thou the mother of thousands of millions, and let thy seed possess the gate of those which hate them" (Genesis 24:60). This is similar to the promise the Lord gave Abraham after the latter had willingly complied with the commandment to offer Isaac as a sacrifice (see Genesis 22:17). It is a promise that Rebekah would be a mother to many and that her seed would have power over evil.

This verse captures the feeling the believers of that day had for the importance of posterity in this life and in eternity. "Be thou the mother of thousands of millions" was the most important thing they could bless her with. The irony of the story is that despite Rebekah's knowledge of the importance of motherhood, despite her desire, twenty barren years passed by. Finally Isaac intreated the Lord (see Genesis 25:21) and Rebekah became pregnant with twins.

Wondering what was happening inside her, Rebekah prayed to the Lord and received a revelation. This tells us more about Rebekah's character. It takes much faith and obedience and practice to learn how to approach the Lord and receive an answer the way Rebekah did. It also tells us a lot about her relationship with the Lord. She did not go to a midwife or a neighbor who had experienced childbirth; instead Rebekah went to the Lord, and he answered her: "Two nations are in thy womb, and two manner of people shall be separated from thy bowels; and the one people shall be stronger than the other people; and the elder shall serve the younger" (Genesis 25:23). Esau was born first, and then Jacob came with his little fist clutching Esau's heel.

The boys grew, and the prophecy Rebekah had been given was fulfilled. Esau strayed from the teachings of the gospel. He married two of the daughters of the land, who worshipped idols, and he sold his birthright to his brother, Jacob. Even though he had despised the birthright and left the covenant, Esau was upset when Jacob received the blessing, and he threatened to kill Jacob. Rebekah urged Jacob to flee to her homeland in Haran in order to escape Esau and to find a worthy wife. At this point we find one of the most poignant verses in all scripture as pertaining to women. Rebekah said to her husband, Isaac, "I am weary of my life because of the daughters of Heth: if Jacob take a wife of the daughters of Heth, such as these which are of the daughters of the land, *what good shall my life do me?"* (Genesis 27:46, italics added.)

Rebekah understood that her stewardship was to offer spiritual as well as physical life. Of course, children still have their agency, and some, such as Esau, choose unwisely. What we should remember is that our salvation is dependent upon our offering what is right, not in their accepting. However, knowing this does not always diminish the pain of parents who love, understand, and offer the gospel only to have their children reject it. This story, however, ended happily in that Jacob did not stray from the covenant and many years later Esau was reconciled with Jacob.

Temporarily Childless

But what of those who do understand the importance of having children and cannot bear children? President Brigham Young said:

> Many of the sisters grieve because they are not blessed with offspring. You will see the time when you will have millions of children around you. If you are faithful to your covenants, you will be mothers of nations. . . . And when you have assisted in peopling one earth, there are millions of earths still in the course of creation. And when they have endured a thousand million times longer than this earth, it is only as it were the beginning of your creations. Be faithful, and if you are not blest with children in this time, you will be hereafter. (*Journal of Discourses* 8:208.)

A woman who places her hope in this promise realizes that even if she does not marry or if she cannot physically bear children, she should be developing the nurturing qualities she will need in order to be an eternal mother. Her calling as help meet gives her the power and opportunities to offer spiritual life. She can serve and sacrifice and learn. She can create and nurture and protect in many ways and thereby mother.

All women whose hearts are pure and who follow the path of righteousness—no matter where that path leads them—will find fulfillment and peace. But no woman can afford to abandon the path of nurturing if she wants to gain exaltation.

Balance through Division of Labor

As a woman prepares and serves as a help meet, she comes to appreciate the division of labor and the balance that exists in the gospel. This is one of the great themes of the Book of Mormon. In the story of the sons of Mosiah, Ammon, Aaron, Omner and Himni went with others on a mission to offer the life-giving ordinances of the gospel to the wicked Lamanites. Their mission was very successful, and many of the Lamanites were converted. These converted Lamanites were so changed by their spiritual birth that they laid down their weapons of war and committed their minds, hearts, strength, and might to the Lord Jesus Christ. It was a glorious conversion, and it was made even more remarkable by righteous women.

The second generation of these Lamanites were brought into the world by loving mothers. Did Ammon, Aaron, Omner, and Himni teach them the gospel? No. Fulfilling their stewardship as helps meet, the Lamanite women gave their time first to learning much, then to expounding the gospel and exhorting each other and the children. By so doing these great mothers raised children who "did not fear death; and they did think more upon the liberty of their fathers than they did upon their lives; yea, they had been taught by their mothers, that if they did not doubt, God would deliver them. And they rehearsed unto me the words of their mothers, saying: We do not doubt our mothers knew it." (Alma 56:47–48.)

It takes more than a family home evening lesson or Primary each week to establish this kind of testimony in the heart of a child. This kind of teaching can only happen when a woman considers mothering her highest priority.

Once again we see a wonderful balance and interdependency in the plan. A man receives the priesthood ordinances from another man. A woman receives the priesthood ordinances from a man. A man receives life from a woman and a woman receives life from another woman. Both man and woman work in partnership with God to perform their stewardships. Both of their stewardships have to do with life. Both are called to give life. A woman is just as important and necessary in helping a man prevent spiritual death through the ordinances as a man is in helping a woman to offer life.

The Importance of a Woman's Calling

The world is trying very hard to make women lose sight of the glorious stewardship which is theirs. To nurture within the flesh of one's own being a spirit child of God is the closest any person comes to godhood while on this earth. To feel life moving within the confines of one's own bones is one of the greatest of all earthly joys. To suffer pain and shed blood to give another life is the most noble of all sacrifices. To give a body, the most precious of all gifts, to a spirit child of God, allowing it to become a soul, is godlike and holy. To teach, train, love, nurture, and protect another soul is the godliest profession on earth. We should never lose sight of the fact that godhood is parenthood perfected. Therefore motherhood is for women the best possible preparation for godhood.

If even one generation of women lose sight of the importance of their calling, years and years of work, teaching, and offering the ordinances comes to a halt and countless numbers of God's children are lost. Brigham Young explained to his daughter Susa Young Gates:

> Daughter, use all your gifts to build up righteousness in the earth. Never use them to acquire name or fame. Never rob your home, nor your children. If you were to become the greatest woman in this world, and your name should be known in every land and clime, and you would fail in your duty as wife and mother, you would wake up on the morning of the first resurrection and find you had failed in everything; but anything you can do after you have satisfied the claims of husband and family will redound to your own honor and to the glory of God. (As quoted in Leonard J. Arrington and Davis Bitton, *The Mormon Experience: A History of the Latter-day Saints* [New York: Alfred A. Knopf, 1979], p. 220.)

Is it any wonder Satan tries so hard to discourage, to belittle, to demean mothering and nurturing? We live in a time when sacrifice is labeled as stupid or unnecessary. We are constantly bombarded with messages that encourage us to get all the pleasure we want from life, to satisfy our own desires and wants, to seek self-fulfillment and to be whatever we want to be. That is not what the Savior of the world did or taught. His life was spent doing for others what they could not do for themselves.

President Spencer W. Kimball said:

Much of the major growth that is coming to the Church in the last days will come because many of the good women of the world (in whom there is often such an inner sense of spirituality) will be drawn to the Church in large numbers. This will happen to the degree that the women of the Church reflect righteousness and articulateness in their lives and to the degree that the women of the Church are seen as distinct and different—in happy ways—from the women of the world. . . .

Thus it will be that female exemplars of the Church will be a significant force in both the numerical and the spiritual growth of the Church in the last days. ("The Role of Righteous Women," *Ensign*, November 1979, pp. 103-4.)

The distinction of "in happy ways" will only come about as men and women understand maleness and femaleness and live the gospel of Jesus Christ as he has admonished them to do.

A Type of the Savior

As women recognize the great privilege that is theirs to offer life, they bring great blessings into the home. As a woman sacrifices to bring children into the world—as she through her very body clothes spirits with coverings of flesh and bone—then continues to sacrifice of her own wants and desires for her family, as she studies and teaches them, to her children she becomes a model of the Savior. It is much easier for a child who has experienced a mother who is there for him, a mother who often places his needs before her own, to come to understand the love the Savior has for us. As a child grows he also comes to understand the depth of this love in that his mother has willingly suffered pain and even shed her blood in order to give him life. This understanding becomes an important bridge that helps the child more easily understand what the Savior did for all mankind.

Whether we are talking about helps meet or mothers, priesthood holders or fathers, the important attainment is not position, status, wants, or self-fulfillment. The important attainments are learning, service, and sacrifice. It is only through these that we can enter into the presence of God. Elder James E. Talmage said, "Mortal eye cannot see nor mind comprehend the beauty, glory, and majesty of a righteous woman made perfect in the celestial kingdom of God" ("The Eternity of Sex," *Young Woman's Journal* 25 [1914]: 602).

No man or woman can gain exaltation without sacrifice. Motherhood and help meet are the means a woman is given to serve and to sacrifice, but only the Spirit can guide each woman to know the exact duties of her mission and how she can best fill her stewardship of offering life. As a woman comes to understand this and to serve well, she establishes her part of the Eden relationship that is essential for a celestial marriage.

In the celestial glory there are three heavens or degrees; and in order to obtain the highest, a man must enter into this order of the priesthood [meaning the new and everlasting covenant of marriage].

—D&C 131:1-2

CHAPTER 7

The Family Quorum

*I*n its original Latin form the word *quorum* meant "of whom." It came to be known as the minimum number of officers and members of a committee or organization that must be present for the valid transaction of business because the expression "of whom" was used in formal commissions to appoint certain persons as members of a group. The Latin wording in such commissions was *"quorum vos unum esse volumus"* meaning, "of whom we will that you be one" (Barry Moser, *Word Mysteries & Histories* [Boston: Houghton Mifflin Company, 1986], p. 198). The word *quorum* appears in scripture only in the Doctrine and Covenants.

As a man and a woman enter into the patriarchal order of the priesthood the words "of whom we will that you be one" apply as they apply to no other body or quorum, in the Church or outside of it. Latter-day Saint usage usually limits the word *quorum* to groups of men holding priesthood office. But a husband and wife who have entered into the patriarchal order of the priesthood form the most important select group necessary for the legal transaction of business. A husband and wife are a chosen body and by definition could justly be called a quorum: the most important type of quorum in all eternity.

A "Mini United Order"

This family quorum is a "mini united order" where all things are held in common and all are given assignments and duties to be performed not for material compensation but for the betterment of the unit. In the family quorum the law of consecration can be lived and practiced to its fullest, sacrifice and service can be performed which help each family member become sanctified. Learning can take place that is significant for eternity.

The Presidency of the Family Quorum

Most priesthood quorums have three people who serve as a presidency over the quorum. The family quorum is no different. When the husband and wife are righteous, the triangular Eden relationship of Deity, husband, and wife serve as the presidency of the family, and often they are the entire unit. Heavenly Father is the head of the home, with the husband presiding under his direction and the wife as an equal partner.

To establish the triangular Eden relationship the "quorum presidency" must be striving for "onement" in three major areas: (1) making the spirit one with the body, (2) making the husband and wife one with each other, and (3) making the couple one with Deity. For the presidency of the family quorum to function well— to teach and do all that they are commanded to do—they should be working on all three of these areas.

"Onement" of Husband and Wife

"Onement" begins as we make the body and spirit one. To do this the spirit has to become stronger than the flesh; or, in other words, we have to follow the promptings of the spirit instead of the promptings of the flesh. One of the great tests of life is whether our body or our spirit will determine our choices in life. As with all other pursuits of "onement," making the body and spirit one is a life-long challenge and not something easily arrived at. The discipline gained in the pursuit, however, is necessary to succeed in the other tests of life, which include "onement" of husband and wife and "onement" of the couple with Jesus Christ.

If there is contention or ill feeling between husband and wife they cannot function in "onement." But what exactly is "onement" of husband and wife? Do a husband and wife have to do and say and feel and think exactly the same thing in order to be one?

The answer can be found in the model of the perfect marriage. Before the Fall, when Adam and Eve were living in the Eden relationship, they were not always together doing the same things. Adam and Eve were each alone when Satan tempted them. They thought and acted independently, adding to the partnership their unique talents and abilities in order to strengthen the partnership. The Eden relationship was one of synergism. In the equation $4+4=$, the answer is eight only if both fours remain on opposites sides of the plus sign. If one four moves to the other side so that it is imposed upon the other four, making only one four, you have merely $4+$ or $+4$; and you lose half of the potential. The very power and strength of "onement" is in remaining on one's own side of the plus sign. In that way the total is eight instead of four. It is the plus sign that combines the two into one. Likewise, we achieve "onement" by adding to each other, not by becoming each other.

The potential, the strength of the marriage unit, comes only when both parties feel confident that their opinions and concerns matter. Both parties must contribute all they can to the relationship. If one or the other dominates, intimidates, or dictates, the effectiveness of the unit is undermined; instead of "onement," there is tyranny. No one person can see everything, hear everything, know everything, perceive everything in its entirety and perfection. President Brigham Young said, "If men know anything, they must know that the Almighty has never yet found a man in mortality that was capable, at the first intimation, at the first impulse, to receive anything in a state of entire perfection" (*Journal of Discourses* 7:14).

When the Lord gave man and woman to each other, he meant that both should see, hear, know, perceive and then share so that each could gain a broader perspective and greater knowledge; they thereby have a more in-depth and complete picture of reality. It is in striving and sharing in this manner that we more fully understand the inspiration and revelation we receive.

A man who demands or encourages his wife to be a silent partner cheats himself. President Spencer W. Kimball said: "We do not want our LDS women to be *silent* partners or *limited* partners in that eternal assignment. Please be a *contributing* and *full* partner." ("Privileges and Responsibilities of Sisters," *Ensign,* November 1978, p. 106.) President John Taylor said, "I am glad there is a little spirit among our sisters, and that they dare say their souls are their own" (as quoted in Leonard J. Arrington and Davis Bitton, *The Mormon Experience: A History of the Latter-day Saints* [New York: Alfred A. Knopf, 1979], p. 220).

Being a support and help to her husband does not mean that a woman is to be his shadow. She is to develop strength, character, and skills; and as Proverbs 31:31 says, she is to be known for her own works. But neither does "onement" mean that a woman can nag, belittle, or demand. She must respect, love, and cherish in order to add to the partnership.

It is important to understand that "onement" between husband and wife is different than being one flesh. The Savior instructed, "Have ye not read, that he which made them at the beginning made them male and female, and said, For this cause shall a man leave father and mother, and shall cleave to his wife: and they twain shall be one flesh? Wherefore they are no more twain, but one flesh. What therefore God hath joined together, let not man put asunder." (Matthew 19:4–6.)

From this scripture we learn: (1) "Them" is two parts, male and female; and "for this cause" a man must cleave to the woman to become "them" instead of only he. (2) One flesh is not something we grow into. It is something we are when we marry. (3) God is the one who joins the couple.

There is a great deal of symbolism in the term "one flesh." The flesh represents the mortal part of us. Often we use the phrase "flesh and blood" to mean the mortal body, so one flesh means one mortal or one person. We use the terms "own flesh and blood" to refer to one's "blood" relatives, usually parents or children. Mortally our flesh is immediately connected to our parents and to our children. There are also links through the flesh that connect us to past and future generations. But when we marry we become connected to another human being that we are not usually related to through "flesh and blood." This connection is made in such a way that it supersedes all other mortal connections. It is not a relationship of two fleshes such as parent and child, but a connection that God himself considers to be one flesh. It is like putting two pieces of a puzzle together so that they are then one picture.

When you look closely into the eyes of your spouse you see yourself. It is a reflection, yes. It happens no matter whose eyes you look into, but when it is your spouse you look at it becomes very symbolic. When you look at your husband or wife you see the part that is your spouse and at the same time in his or her eyes you see the part that is you. Only as you see yourself incorporated in your spouse and your spouse incorporated in you do you see yourself completely, wholly. What you do or say or think about your spouse you do or say or think about yourself. You are connected, you are related, you are one flesh; therefore, in marriage selfishness means literally cutting yourself in halves and caring for only one half of what is you.

The challenge, then, is to make the "one flesh" of mortality eternally one by having the union sealed by the Holy Spirit of Promise. Too often we think having been married in the temple is the goal and that once the ceremony is over it is accomplished. But that is not enough. Temple marriage is only a beginning. "All covenants, contracts, bonds, obligations, oaths, vows, performances, connections, associations, or expectations, that are not made and entered into and sealed by the Holy Spirit of Promise . . . are of no efficacy, virtue, or force in and after the resurrection from the dead; for all contracts that are not made unto this end have an end when men are dead" (D&C 132:7).

The goal is to be sealed by the Holy Spirit of Promise. The ceremony only opens the door to the accomplishment of the goal. Being sealed by the Holy Spirit of Promise can only happen if a couple becomes one in faith, belief, purpose, and power. Becoming one flesh occurs when you become a unit, but becoming "at one" is not so automatic. "Onement" is what a couple achieves as they strive to be like God. "Onement" must be worked for and is necessary before the couple can be sealed by the Holy Spirit of Promise.

So far we have talked a lot about "onement", but even that is contingent upon proper balance. Both the man and the woman have been given specific duties whereby they can achieve the goal of "onement." Both the man and the woman work in partnership with the Spirit and the Savior; both have primary responsibility to perform those duties in their own families.

The accompanying diagram helps us to analyze the triangular Eden relationship. From studying the ties that bind the triangle we learn a lot about how "onement" happens.

GODHEAD
authors of the plan of salvation

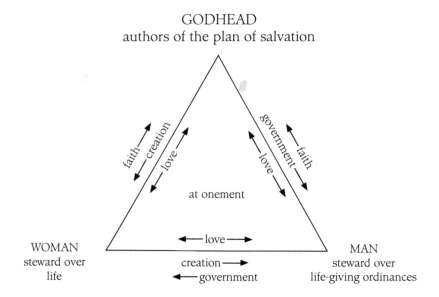

The "onement" we are striving for occurs when all the proper connections are made in the triangle. We are then connected, made one, not because all our duties, thoughts, and actions are the same but because our hearts are the same. Love becomes the binding, all-encompassing connection that holds the triangle together. The Eden relationship can only be achieved if each person works in partnership with the others in the triangle.

In order for "onement" to happen we must all participate in the Atonement by doing all we can to bring about "at-one-ment" or unity. The Savior did and does his part; now we must do ours. The Church exists to teach us, assist us, and guide us. "Onement" happens by doing; and doing is concerned not with doctrines, procedures, or principles (though all of these are important), but with relationships. These important relationships first occur at home and in the family.

"Onement" is so important that you don't have to look far to see the many ways that Satan attacks in order to stop "onement" from occurring. His goal is to establish chaos and discord. He uses tools such as selfishness, discouragement, fear, and laziness to break apart, to sever, to destroy.

One of the most fundamental tools Satan uses that isn't so often recognized became evident after Adam and Eve partook of the forbidden fruit and their "onement" with Deity was severed. Adam and Eve heard the voice of the Lord, a thing that had happened many times before, but this time instead of anxiously greeting the Lord they ran and hid from him. The Lord called to them the soul-searching question, "Where goest thou?" (Moses 4:15.)

Why were Adam and Eve suddenly afraid? They had never run away before. But the Fall had made Adam and Eve different, and they were afraid because of that difference. Just when Adam and Eve needed God most, just when they should have been seeking him, they ran away from him.

Satan uses the tool of fear of differences whenever there are natural boundaries. He uses this tool not only to separate man and woman from God but also to separate man and woman from each other. Yes, we are different, but sometimes we dwell so much on the differences that we forget that we are also very much alike.

During the seventeen years my husband and I were raising only daughters, almost everyone I met told me how very different boys were from girls. By the time I finally had a son I was expecting a totally different species! Because of all the well-meaning instruction, the shock for me came not in finding out how different boys and girls are, but how much alike they are.

Often as husbands and wives we would be greatly helped if we would forget about the overemphasized differences between men and women and remember that they are more alike than they are different. Men and women both need to be loved. Both need to feel capable and worthwhile and wanted. Both have egos. Both need to be understood. Both have dreams and goals to work toward and a divine mission to fulfill. Both have the same spiritual needs, and both need to have faith in Jesus Christ.

"Onement" with Deity

This leads us to the third area of "onement." The husband and wife must be one with Jesus Christ. All faith centers in the Savior and is essential in attaining a celestial marriage and administering the family quorum.

Some men and women have a difficult time understanding the relationship between following a husband in righteousness and centering faith in the Savior. Occasionally a husband, usually in very subtle ways, encourages his wife to be spiritually dependent on him or to place her faith in him instead of in Jesus Christ. For some women this is a dilemma. They see this difference in sources of faith and government as a discrepancy; and, if they remain unable to reconcile the discrepancy, they place their faith in their husbands instead of in the Savior.

But this need not be. A husband's call to preside is an order of jurisdiction to be followed to keep chaos from reigning on the earth. But faith does not come through government. A husband is a wife's priesthood leader, but he is not her Savior. Both the husband and the wife need to have faith in Jesus Christ and should give their first allegiance to him and to God the Father by following the Holy Ghost. If a man, however subtly, encourages a woman to place her faith in him instead of in Deity, he could very well be keeping her and himself from exaltation. A woman who finds it easier to place her faith in her husband than to develop faith in Jesus Christ may be risking all that eternity has to offer.

President Ezra Taft Benson said: "The scripture says, 'Honour thy father and thy mother' (Exodus 20:12; see also Mosiah 13:20). Sometimes one must choose to honor a Heavenly Father over a mortal father. We should give God, the Father of our spirits, an exclusive preeminence in our lives. He has a prior parental claim on our eternal welfare, *ahead of all other ties that may bind us here or hereafter.*" ("The Great Commandment—Love the Lord," *Ensign,* May 1988, p. 5, italics added.)

As important as the marriage relationship is, as important as it is to be one flesh, a man's and a woman's first allegiance is to God the Father and Jesus Christ, in whom all faith must center. A woman is to follow her husband in righteousness. A husband who demands any more than that endangers his own salvation; and a woman who blindly allows a man to indulge in selfish or unrighteous practices does not love him enough to care about his eternal welfare. We are each given to the other to help not to hinder the other. This does not mean that a husband has the right to contend with his spouse, or vice versa. Contention is of the devil. What it does mean is that we should seek the guidance of the Spirit and use love, patience, wisdom, and influence to encourage a spouse, realizing that we will be held accountable if we merely sit back and let the spouse "do his/her thing," all the while knowing that it is wrong.

Problem-Solving and Decision-Making

Once again we see the balance that is part of the gospel plan. As a husband and wife function in the Eden relationship, decisions need to be made and conflicts and disagreements arise. It would have been easier if Lehi had been inspired to say, "There must needs be an opposition in all things except marriage," but he didn't. However, there are ways to solve our problems and reach decisions, ways that help alleviate the contention and hurt feelings that can occur.

When faced with a problem or a decision we can hold an "executive session of the family council." A good pattern to follow in this meeting would be to (1) calmly explain the problem, (2) without argument or condemnation discuss the options that are open to us, and (3) decide upon the solution that accomplishes the most good for the most people involved.

It doesn't matter who is to blame, so arguing about that wastes time. Ranting, raving, screaming, condemning, hurting or belittling have never solved a problem. Those things are contrary to all that is necessary for "onement." When we analyze the things that we as husbands and wives get upset about, they are seldom eternally significant. The most important thing is to do what is right at any given moment despite what happened in the preceding moment.

But the gospel offers us more to help with these "executive sessions of the family council." The scriptures tell us that "in the mouth of two or three witnesses shall every word be established" (2 Corinthians 13:1; D&C 6:28; D&C 128:3). As a husband and wife turn in times of decision or disagreement to our Father in fasting and prayer, they are both entitled to know what his will is. When a man receives a prompting or answer to his prayer he has one witness, but when his wife receives the same answer he has the promised two witnesses. When a wife receives an answer to prayer and her husband has received the same answer, she also has two witnesses. With two witnesses both the man and the woman can move forward with total confidence and faith that they have received the will of the Father.

This is the ideal. When applied, it is effective and builds a strong relationship in which mutual respect and love flourish. It is almost always possible to fast and pray concerning big decisions, such as where to live or how many children the Lord wants us to have. But in our human condition time often becomes a pressure so that a period of fasting is not feasible. What do we do then?

Perhaps a wife has a Church meeting she is to attend. In accepting the call to serve, she has committed herself to do all that is required of her to fulfill her calling. In a calling such as an auxiliary presidency this includes such things as attending leadership meetings. She wants to go, feels strongly the responsibility to go, intends to go, but her husband tells her he has made a commitment that the couple will go to the temple with the elders quorum presidency on the same night as her leadership meeting. First they discuss the problem. She explains that the leadership meeting is only quarterly and that in order to function in her calling she needs to be at the meeting to receive information that will be provided. He says he doesn't like to go to the temple alone when all the others will have their wives there, and that temple work is important.

After a discussion of wants and desires, they should pray about it (even with "moment's notice" decisions prayer is always possible!); and those who have been seeking the ideal and who have practiced obtaining two witnesses may come to agreement after prayer. Others may still have a problem. At this point the husband who presides must make a decision, but in so doing he must be very careful. Presiding does not mean that his desires are always the *right* ones. If he insists she accompany him out of selfish reasons or because he always assumes that what he has to do is more important than what she has to do, he will be held responsible for the decision and for her not attending her meeting. But if after sincere prayer he comes to the conclusion that she should be with him at the temple, he should state what he has determined, and then it is her turn to decide. If she then refuses to go, she will be responsible.

Still we see the balance in that both parties have the privilege of calling upon God for help. Each has agency. Each must accept responsibility for his or her choices. Each person can discuss and express his or her feelings and desires, but when a decision is made there should finally be unity and "onement." If the husband goes to the temple alone, all the while mad that his wife wouldn't come, or if she goes all the while mad that he made her come, their outer actions are one but they are not one. It is in the feelings and intents of the heart that "onement" comes.

There could be more than one right solution to the problem. The problem could even repeat itself and the right solution be different each time. The important thing to remember is that a decision carries with it a consequence and that the right to preside carries with it responsibility, because at some point in time an accounting will have to be made as to how well a husband followed the will of the Lord while presiding. Likewise wives will have to account for how well they obeyed their husbands' righteous requests.

When we realize the importance of the family quorum, we recognize that the instructions given for the governance of priesthood quorums as found in the Doctrine and Covenants are also very good advice for family quorums. From this advice we can learn a lot about how to make terrestrial family life into celestial family life. The Lord gave instructions as follows to the quorums of the First Presidency, Twelve, and the Seventy in this dispensation: "And every decision made by either of these quorums must be by the unanimous voice of the same; that is, every member in each quorum must be agreed to its decisions, in order to make their decisions of the same power or validity one with the other. A majority may form a quorum when circumstances render it impossible to be otherwise." (D&C 107:27–28.)

If both the husband and the wife center their faith in Jesus Christ and give him and God the Father the first place in their hearts, they will be directed and blessed by the Spirit with the answers they need. Instead of protecting their own best interests or playing emotional games, they can know God's will and follow it. They can be unanimous.

Section 107 goes on to say: "The decisions of these quorums, or either of them, are to be made in all righteousness, in holiness, and lowliness of heart, meekness and long suffering, and in faith, and virtue, and knowledge, temperance, patience, godliness, brotherly kindness and charity; because the promise is, if these things abound in them they shall not be unfruitful in the knowledge of the Lord" (D&C 107:30–31).

As the husband and wife become one by abiding by the advice in section 107, it becomes much easier to administer the affairs of the family. A husband and wife pray together. They discuss and decide together. They share everything in a "mini-united order" or a condition where all things are held in common. This means that they hold back no secrets. A man does not "protect" his wife by keeping the family finances a secret no matter how dismal the picture. A woman does not "protect" the husband by keeping children's school behavior secret. If either one of the marriage partners is trying to shoulder burdens alone, he is defeating the very purpose of marriage. Love is not hiding information from a spouse; love is trusting the spouse and helping him to deal with information. There can be no "onement" in concealment. If we are the one information is being withheld from, we should examine and rectify any of our behavior that would cause a spouse not to trust us with information.

When both parties have all the available information, it is much easier to make decisions. One man thought he was helping his wife after the birth of a handicapped son. The husband instructed the bishop that the wife was needed to care for the son and that he should not give her any callings. The husband also felt that the wife had her hands so full he shouldn't bother her with matters like finances or decisions; he took care of all the business affairs of the home. His intentions were good, but he literally shut her off from the world so that all she was doing was caring for the handicapped child, cleaning, and cooking.

After a few years a doctor told the husband that if he didn't "let the wife out of her prison" she would have a nervous breakdown. Rather than our segregating and shielding in such circumstances, almost all difficult situations are made better by sharing. If this husband had shared information and relieved some of the burden of the tedious household chores and care of the child so that his wife could do Church work and pursue a few other outside interests, she would not have had the emotional problems she did. A mother and father should make the family a first priority, but we all need outside influences, stimulation, and variety of activity to help us grow and to give us additional feelings of competence and worth.

Pitfalls of Cultural Tradition

It is interesting to get to know couples who have chosen each other through the direction of the Lord. Usually it is easy to see how they complement each other. This is another of the beauties of the plan, but one we too often misunderstand. Too often we let cultural traditions dictate a husband-wife relationship. Nowhere in the scriptures does it say that the husband should handle all the financial matters. Nowhere does it say that a woman should change all the diapers. (I once heard a man say that a husband could not be one with a wife if he never changed diapers!) Instead of letting cultural traditions dictate our actions, it is important that each couple determine where the strengths and failings of their unit lie and then assign duties according to strengths instead of tradition. It is not a sign of weakness in a man if his wife handles the finances. It is not a sign of inadequacy in a woman if her husband does the cooking. Each partner should contribute his best and at the same time keep the other informed as to what he is doing, so that each partner can help make important decisions.

Cultural traditions sometimes threaten the family unit in the vital spiritual area. It seems that too often we concentrate on separating priesthood and help meet instead of uniting them. While there are some very distinct and important separations concerning authority and government, there are also some very important principles such as faith, knowledge, and love wherein priesthood and helps meet should function together. Certainly, both women and men need to study the gospel, for example.

One young mother woke up on the morning scheduled for the blessing of her new baby to discover that her four-year-old was too sick to go to Church. When she told her husband that they would have to postpone the blessing, his reply was: "Why? You don't need to be there; only I do." There can be no onement with that kind of division. Obviously, at any blessing or ordinance the combined faith and love of the husband and wife are important even though only one of them is voice in the ordinance.

We must be careful that we do not let cultural traditions de-
prive us of the power, faith, and love that being one flesh was
meant to give. The faith of two is greater than the faith of one; and
holding the priesthood is not a requirement for faith.

Remember the Real Goal

We talk a lot in the Church about creating strong families. We
so often describe ways and means of establishing family unity,
however, that sometimes we forget the principles behind the tech-
niques; we forget the purpose. We encourage unity through family
vacations and recreation, and suddenly vacations and recreation
become the goal instead of the means to the goal. While campers
and boats and cabins and other material things can encourage
family unity, they are not essential to it. The goal is to return to the
presence of God as a family. If the material things are affordable,
by all means use them for family unity; if they are not, we can't afford to forsake the nurturing, the loving, the serving, in order to
work more hours to buy the campers and boats and vacations.

The trials and tests of the family unit are many and are unique
to each family. The most important thing is to draw close to the
Spirit so that we can recognize our own challenges and then know
how to meet them.

Elder Bruce R. McConkie said:

I think that the noblest concept that can enter the heart of man is
the fact that the family unit continues in eternity. I do not think
that one can conceive of a more glorious concept than that—building, of course, on the foundation of the atoning sacrifice of the
Lord Jesus. Celestial marriage is the thing that opens the door to
eternal life in our Father's kingdom. *If we can pass the probationary
experiences that prevail and exist in the family unit,* then the Lord
will say to us at some future day, "Well done, thou good and
faithful servant: . . . enter thou into the joy of the Lord" (Matthew
25:21). (*1977 Devotional Speeches of the Year, BYU Devotional and
Twelve-Stake Fireside Adresses* [Provo, Utah: Brigham Young University Press, 1978], p. 174, italics added.)

We must not lose sight of the fact that the family quorum is the
most important unit in the Church. When the members of the

Godhead become partners in the marriage, when first allegiance is given to our Heavenly Father, when faith centers in Jesus Christ and diligence and heed is given to the promptings of the Holy Ghost, the husband-and-wife relationship blossoms into the eternally rewarding relationship it should be. The parts—man, woman, and God—become a whole. Four plus four suddenly equals sixteen instead of eight because of the extra power on all sides of the equation. Synergism takes place that makes the whole more powerful than the parts could ever hope to be. Then and only then can the family quorum become a celestial unit, an eternal husband and wife.

But whoso committeth adultery with a woman lacketh
understanding: he that doeth it destroyeth his own soul.
                                                    —Proverbs 6:32

CHAPTER 8

The Sacred
Gift

I have seen sorrow in the eyes of begging children who called "bak-
sheesh" while stretching stained hands toward me. I will never
forget the large brown eyes that weren't afraid to hold onto my
gaze or the accusing way they held that gaze. The sorrow was
deep, physical; but there was also a love planted there by mothers
who could give little else, a love that blanketed the sorrow, easing
its sharpness and terror.

I have seen sorrow in the eyes of one dying. Those were shal-
low, blue eyes, yet the sorrow was the same. It, too, contained pain
and distress, but that sorrow was comforted by a blanket of hope
that soon some strange event called death would rip away the sorrow and bring peace.

But the sorrow I remember most was in the eyes of a young
mother as she tearfully told how much she wanted another baby.
While pregnant with her third child, she had made a decision not
to have any more children. She had missed the ski season for so
many years because of pregnancy and caring for an infant that she
couldn't bear the thoughts of having another child. Now the third

child was growing, no longer a toddler, and the mother would never again miss the ski season because of pregnancy. But as she looked into my eyes I saw sorrow that I had never seen before—comfortless, stark, terrifying sorrow. "I want another baby so badly," she said. "And I can't have one."

That day an awareness of how very precious the gift of procreation is began to intensify within me. The great gift of helping God in the creation of mortal bodies cannot be taken lightly, because the consequences are far-reaching and eternally significant. The gift must be used and the gift must be protected.

Chastity Is for the Married Too

Too often we think discussions on chastity are for those not yet married. Too often we think that after marriage chastity means avoiding adultery. But for Latter-day Saints chastity must reach much further than that.

In all of the holy scriptures the words *chastity* and *chaste* appear only seven times. The Lord has chosen to teach us about chastity by telling us what we are not to do, unlike a commandment such as "Honor thy father and thy mother," which tells us what to do. However, whether a commandment says "do" or "do not" it carries with it an implied "inverted" commandment. When God says, "Thou shalt have none other gods before me" (Deuteronomy 5:7), the inverted commandment is, "Thou shalt put me first." When God says, "Thou shalt not take the name of the Lord thy God in vain," the implied commandment is, "Thou shalt take the name of the Lord thy God with reverent intent." When God says, "Keep the sabbath day to sanctify it" (Deuteronomy 5:12), the inversion of the commandment is, "Do not do anything that would destroy the sanctity of the sabbath." When God says: "Thou shalt not kill. Neither shalt thou commit adultery" (Deuteronomy 5:17–18), the implied commandment seems to be, "Thou shalt protect life and also protect the sacred way life is given."

The dictionary describes *chastity* as "the state or quality of being pure." The Latin source of the word, *castus,* means pure. When we understand that chastity is purity, we realize that after marriage the concept of chastity expands rather than diminishes. Included in the protection of procreation's sacredness, chastity after marriage means total fidelity to one's spouse and using this great power of creation purely, the way it was intended to be used.

Chastity: Protecting
Sacredness of Sexual Union

Chastity is protecting the sacredness of the way life begins. The holiness and sacredness of the sexual union of man and wife cannot be given enough emphasis. It is more than just a relationship; it is a covenant. President Joseph Fielding Smith said, "Nothing should be held in greater sacredness and honor than the covenant by which the spirits of men—the offspring of God in the spirit—are privileged to come into this world in mortal tabernacles" (*The Way to Perfection* [Salt Lake City: Genealogical Society of Utah, 1946], pp. 233–34).

By definition, a covenant is "a binding and solemn compact, agreement, contract, or mutual promise between God and a single person or a group of chosen persons" (Bruce R. McConkie, *Mormon Doctrine* 2nd ed. [Salt Lake City: Bookcraft, 1966], p. 166). What is the covenant or agreement of the sexual union? To be one flesh. As a married couple consummate their legal marriage they are covenanting to think of the spouse as themselves, to care for the spouse, to give to the spouse, to help the spouse return to the Father. Sexual union should be a deeply spiritual experience of great love and meaning and symbolism. It is an actual bonding wherein twain literally become one. This is one reason why this union is not to be taken lightly. The apostle Paul warned: "What? know ye not that he which is joined to an harlot is one body? for two, saith he, shall be one flesh." (1 Corinthians 6:16.)

When a person begins to catch this vision of marriage making two people one flesh, he realizes why divorce is so terrible and should only be an alternative in extreme circumstances. Divorce is the breaking of a covenant. Not just a covenant between a man and a woman, but a covenant between a man, a woman, and God. It isn't uncommon today to hear of people divorcing because they say they just don't love each other any more. But in the scriptures love is not something we "fall" into; rather, it is something we choose. The Lord has said, "Thou shalt love thy wife with all thy heart, and shalt cleave unto her and none else" (D&C 42:22). The same commandment applies to a wife.

In Old Testament times, often love was not the prerequisite for marriage. Rather, parents selected marriage partners. Frequently the couple had never seen each other before the ceremony. But they understood that they could make the marriage one of love. Even after the deception Laban practiced on Jacob, the latter did not say, "I do not love Leah, I want to divorce her." He stayed married to her, took care of her. In many biblical marriages, such as Isaac and Rebekah's, the love came after the ceremony as the couple struggled to establish the Eden relationship.

We can be thankful that custom has changed, but we can also learn much from our biblical friends. If a marriage is no longer full of love, the answer is not necessarily divorce; the answer could very well be repentance. In some cases, however, one partner is willing to repent, but the other is not. Then the Spirit may direct one to seek divorce; but if he or she is seeking exaltation, a person must be very sure it is the Spirit that is directing and not his or her own selfishness.

President Joseph F. Smith said, "Sexual union is lawful in wedlock, and, *if participated in with right intent is honorable and sanctifying.*" ("Unchastity the Dominant Evil of the Age," *Improvement Era,* June 1917, p. 739, italics added.) We are told in the Doctrine and Covenants that "the spirit and the body are the soul of man" (D&C 88:15). Therefore, if a person joins to his body another body (becomes one flesh), it is not just the bodies but the souls that are affected, changed, altered by that addition. It is important, therefore, that the addition be a righteous one and that the unioin be legal and lawful.

Not only are the laws about chastity and murder adjacent to one another in the Ten Commandments (see Exodus 20:13–14), but under the Mosaic law the penalty for murder and for committing adultery was the same; death. Anyone who refused to protect the sacredness of the way life begins paid the same price as one who would not allow another's life its full natural extension. He forfeited his own life. How very seriously the Lord regards the law of chastity! No wonder Satan hurls his most vicious, snide attacks in an effort to undermine the law of chastity. Elder Boyd K. Packer explained: "[Satan] knows that this power of creation is not just an incident in the plan, but is a key to it. He knows that if he can entice you to use this power prematurely, to use it too soon, *or to misuse it in any way*, you may well lose your opportunities for eternal progression." (Conference Report, Stockholm Sweden Area Conference, 1974, p. 83, italics added.)

We mentioned in chapter 6 that God gave to Eve her spirit, or breath of lives. A woman's body contains within it the first cell, the potential for many mortal bodies. "The million or two primordial egg cells already formed in the female's ovaries at the time of birth are more than sufficient. Assuming roughly 400 menstrual cycles during a woman's fertile years, this means that not even every thousandth primordial egg cell will mature into a fertilizable ovum." (Lennart Nilsson, *A Child Is Born* [New York: Delacourt Press/Seymour Lawrence, 1977], p. 30.) What happens to the hundreds of thousands of ova never used in a woman's lifetime? We do not know. We are told that our bodies will be restored to their perfect state in the resurrection. Does that mean the ovum will also be restored? Again, we do not know. But it is interesting to contemplate why so many are given when so few are used. As I have explored the questions, even though I have found no answers, my awe and my understanding of why chastity is so important have increased.

We are told in the scriptures that "Adam fell that men might be; and men are, that they might have joy" (2 Nephi 2:25). The gift of procreation is one of the keys to joy, and those who misuse or abuse it deny themselves the very purpose of life. Elder Boyd K. Packer said: "Within your body is the power to beget life, to share in creation. The only legitimate expression of that power is within the covenant of marriage. *The worthy use of it is the very key to your happiness.*" ("To Young Women and Men," *Ensign*, May 1989, p. 54, italics added.)

Satan and his premortal followers cannot have a mortal body. They cannot have a true counterpart and be one flesh with that person in order to make themselves complete, whole. They cannot pass on to others the great gift of mortal flesh and blood. Because they cannot do these things they will never have joy. Therefore in their selfish, malicious ways Satan and his followers try to keep us from joy and growth.

In Proverbs we read: "Can a man take fire in his bosom, and his clothes not be burned? Can one go upon hot coals, and his feet not be burned? . . . But whoso comitteth adultery with a woman lacketh understanding: he that doeth it destroyeth his own soul." (Proverbs 6:27–28, 32.)

The physical union is not just a covenant between man and woman. In a holy and sacred way, God is also part of the covenant. Anyone who tampers with that covenant or takes it lightly runs the risk that he will pay with his life—his spiritual life. This means that even within the marriage relationship impure practices are to be avoided. The sexual act is intended to be sacred and should never be degraded or abused. Instead, we should diligently strive to do all we can to protect and keep sacred the covenant by which life is given.

Chastity: Fidelity in Marriage

Fidelity means faithfulness to duties, obligations, and vows. It is interesting to note some of the synonyms of the word *fidelity:* allegiance, devotion, loyalty, adherence, attachment, faithfulness, honesty, integrity. Each one of these qualities becomes an important key to a good marriage. When we realize that chastity is more than not committing adultery, we realize that chastity in marriage means fidelity in all one's thoughts, words, and actions.

Infidelity in thoughts, words, or actions disturbs and may destroy any bonds of "onement." It severs "onement" with God and with spouse, and obviously is a contradiction to the very idea of the spirit and body being one through the spirit ruling the body. Fidelity and chastity, on the other hand, allow the spirit to become strong, to rule.

The Savior, when instructing the Nephites after his resurrection, said: "Behold, it is written by them of old time, that thou shalt not commit adultery; but I say unto you, that whosoever looketh on a woman, to lust after her, hath committed adultery already in his heart. Behold, I give unto you a commandment, that ye suffer none of these things to enter into your heart; for it is better that ye should deny yourselves of these things, wherein ye will take up your cross, than that ye should be cast into hell." (3 Nephi 12:27–30.)

Too often we underestimate, take for granted, or don't notice the strength given to those who live this higher law of chastity.

Who would we serve and sacrifice for? How would we learn to be gods?

Our own physical bodies were the reward for keeping our first estate. They are ours because of our obedience. The great reward of this second estate will be the completion of this body: becoming one flesh with a counterpart in order to have seed for all eternity. The reward is not only a completed unit but the gift to eternally give others life.

President Joseph Fielding Smith taught: "Some of the functions in the celestial body will not appear in the terrestrial body, neither in the telestial body, and *the power of procreation will be removed*" (*Doctrines of Salvation*, comp. Bruce R. McConkie, 3 vols. [Salt Lake City: Bookcraft, 1954–56], 2:288).

One reason why Adam agreed to partake of the forbidden fruit was so that he and Eve could have children. One of the greatest of the promises made to Abraham and Sarah was that they would have seed, or children. "And I will make thee exceeding fruitful, and I will make nations of thee, and kings shall come out of thee" (Genesis 17:6). To be able to have spirit children is the reward of the highest state of the celestial kingdom. Our endeavors here are tests as well as preparation and education for the hereafter, and parenting is one of the greatest preparatory events. At a BYU Education Week class Chauncey Riddle said that couples who do not want children in this life will not be able to have children in the next life. That is a startling thought, but when analyzed it rings true. It seems reasonable that those who for selfish reasons refuse to bring children into the world give up the right to inherit the highest degree in the celestial glory, where those who attain that reward will be able to have children hereafter.

President Joseph F. Smith said: "In 1 Timothy 2:13–15, we are told that 'Adam was first formed, then Eve. And Adam was not deceived, but the woman being deceived was in the transgression. Notwithstanding she shall be saved in childbearing, if they continue in faith and charity and holiness with sobriety.' Can she be saved without child-bearing? She indeed takes an awful risk if she wilfully disregards what is a pronounced requirement of God. How shall she plead her innocence when she is not innocent? How shall she excuse her guilt when it is fastened upon her?" (*Gospel Doctrine* [Salt Lake City: Deseret Book, 1939], pp. 288–89.) The Joseph Smith Translation of the New Testament changes 1 Timothy 2:15 to read "Notwithstanding *they* shall be saved in child-bearing" (italics added).

But it often turns out that to want children and to have children are not the same thing. For those who would have children if they could, the desire of the heart is the most important thing to the Lord. Just as surely as priesthood may be obtained by all worthy men, in the celestial glory parenthood will be given to all worthy couples.

Prophets throughout the years have cautioned us to use wisdom when bringing children into the world. The mother's health and proper care for the children brought into the world are as important as the number of children. Nevertheless it isn't a doctor who should decide whether a couple should have more children. His or her opinion should be considered, but it is the Lord to whom the couple should turn for confirmation of a decision.

The important thing is not how many children we have but that we bring into the world all that the Lord wants us to bring. For some that may be one or two, or even none, while for others it may mean thirteen! Each couple must prayerfully ask the Lord for answers to such eternally significant questions. The problem today is that too many couples are determining the size of their family not by asking the Lord but because the material things of the world or activities or careers are what they want to spend their lives on. They do not understand that the eventual sorrow such a decision will bring is painful and comfortless.

Lasting Source Provides Lasting Joy

Joy is not found in the things of the world but only its counterfeit, pleasure. If we look to the things of the world to give us joy we lose all possibility of finding it. On a hot summer day a Popsicle might bring momentary relief from the heat, but it is soon gone. Likewise the things of this world will melt away. Unless joy is derived from a lasting source, joy will not be lasting.

If we want lasting joy we must live the law of chastity. We must protect the sacredness of the way life begins, we must love our spouses with complete fidelity, we must responsibly use this power God has given us to provide his children with bodies. As Elder Boyd K. Packer said: "The power of creation—or may we say procreation—is not just an incidental part of the plan: it is essential to it. Without it the plan could not proceed. The misuse of it may disrupt the plan." ("Why Stay Morally Clean," *Ensign,* July 1972, p. 111.)

As we enter into the covenant of marriage, we covenant to help our Father in Heaven and his Son Jesus Christ to accomplish the work of the plan of salvation.

President Ezra Taft Benson answered the question, "How did Adam bring his descendants into the presence of the Lord?" with a powerful answer:

> Adam and his descendants entered into the priesthood order of God. Today we would say they went to the House of the Lord and received their blessings.
>
> The order of priesthood spoken of in the scriptures is sometimes referred to as the patriarchal order because it came down from father to son.
>
> But this order is otherwise described in modern revelation as an order of family government where a man and woman enter into a covenant with God—just as did Adam and Eve—to be sealed for eternity, *to have posterity,* and to do the will and work of God throughout their mortality. ("What I Hope You Will Teach Your Children About the Temple," *Ensign,* August 1985, p. 9, italics added.)

The sacred gift of procreation is one of the keys to the accomplishment of the purposes of the patriarchal order of the priesthood. It is one of the great keys to joy. Only by being pure and chaste can we fully gain the spiritual power and strength we need in order to establish an Eden relationship.

And they were married, and given in marriage, and were blessed according to the multitude of the promises which the Lord had made unto them.

—4 Nephi 1:11

CHAPTER 9

Establishing the Triangular Eden Relationship

Carl and I had not been married many years when I attended priesthood meeting to witness his setting apart as elders quorum president. I left as soon as the blessing was over, followed by the man who had just been released as president. When we reached the parking lot he stopped me. "Whatever you do," he said with tears in his eyes, "support your husband. Don't complain about what he does or the time he is away from you, and you will both be blessed." All of us have known priesthood leaders who were released, or who were not as effective as they could have been, because their wives would not support them.

On another occasion my husband and I attended a dinner party where we were seated at a table with three other couples, none of whom we knew. The man to our left was a religion teacher, but the place where his wife should have been was empty. Each course was served to her place, and he kept saying that she would be there shortly, but she never came. We finally asked if there was a problem, and he explained that his wife was in the ladies' room with one of her frequent migraine headaches.

As the evening progressed we began to get acquainted with the others at the table. When it was discovered that I had a large family and did some writing, someone asked, "How do you find time to write?" At that time Carl was taking over the house and children every Saturday morning for three hours while I wrote. When the man to our left heard this, he abruptly dropped the fork full of food he was about to put into his mouth. "It would be a cold day in hell," he said, "before I would tend children while *my* wife wrote."

Marriage a Supportive Partnership

What a sad commentary it is that so many people do not understand the importance of not only their own but also their spouse's callings and mission in life! What unhappiness is caused because people fail to realize that part of their obligation in life is to help the spouse fulfill his or her obligations! On the other hand, what a blessed couple it is who know and understand how to support and help each other along life's journey so that each one achieves and grows and learns and serves to whatever extent they need to and can!

There is a happy medium that we all need to find. I once heard a woman remark that she didn't need to study the scriptures because her husband knew them so well. She was wrong about that. Salvation is first an individual and then a family effort. Both men and women must individually gain the necessary knowledge and power in order to progress spiritually.

A man once told me that his wife had been born with so much faith that she had enough for both of them. He may not have meant this seriously, but some act as if it were true in their case. In reality, faith is an internal power. A wife's car might be full of gas but it doesn't help her husband's car go. She may share a gallon, which may get him a few miles, but the long journey to eternal life requires more faith than can be siphoned from another's tank.

In the beginning God created the lands and the waters, the lights in the firmament, and the seeds and all manner of vegetation. He created the day and the night, the fowls of the air, the fish of the sea, and all the beasts of the earth and after each of these five days of creation, "God saw that it was good" (Genesis 1:10, 12, 18,

21, 25). But on the sixth day God created man, and he said, *"It is not good* that the man should be alone" (Genesis 2:18, italics added).

Most members of the Church realize that one reason why it is not good for man to be alone is that a man cannot receive exaltation without a woman at his side. Likewise a woman cannot receive exaltation without a man at her side. But what some of us fail to realize is that attaining the highest degree of glory in the celestial kingdom requires that we know why the spouse is at our side.

Husband and wife were meant to be partners. Even the word we use when entering this partnership in celestial marriage—the word *sealed*—emphasizes the concept of unity. Many husbands and wives, however, even though married and living together, remain very much alone. God considers them to be one flesh, a unit; but they do not function as such. Either one or the other or both have an inadequate blueprint of what marriage is supposed to be. It is when we catch sight of the balance, the true blueprint, that we really begin to grow in our marriages.

God intended married couples to be one flesh in order to give each individual more strength, more power, more talents, more ability. But we receive more only as we work together, complementing and strengthening each other by giving—not taking, for taking depletes the relationship. It also only happens as we turn to God and strive diligently to live his laws. Only as this whole and complete unit of man, woman, and God is accomplished, as the triangular eternal unit is established, will God be able to say, "It is good, man is not alone."

In the Joseph Smith Translation of Genesis, the Prophet added several things that help us understand how Adam and Eve reestablished the Eden relationship they had enjoyed before the Fall. Two examples are: "And Adam ceased not to call upon God; and Eve also his wife" (JST, Genesis 5:3). "And Adam and Eve blessed the name of God; and they made all things known unto their sons and their daughters" (JST, Genesis 4:12). From these and other verses found in the JST Genesis account and the book of Moses account, we learn that (1) Adam and Eve learned from the Lord and taught their children and each other (see Moses 5:10–12); (2) they served each other and the Lord (see Moses 5:1, 6–8); (3) they called upon the Lord and did what he told them to do (Moses 5:4, 6–8).

These are the same things we need to do if we are going to establish an Eden relationship in our lives. Let us examine each of these in more detail.

Learn and Teach

Adam and Eve learned from the Lord and taught their children and each other.

Because of their unique life experiences, men and women can add much to each other's understanding of the gospel. In a general sense men and women see things differently. I remember in a college psychology class discussing how the average woman upon entering a room sees things one by one, taking in the detail, while the average man takes in the whole setting as one picture. As individuals, disregarding gender, we see things differently because of the conditioning resulting from our life experiences. This means that as two people observe and then share, they gain a clearer perception of truth. With this shared view the journey through life becomes not only easier but also more enjoyable, and each has a better chance of arriving at the truth.

An example of this happened a few years ago while I was studying the book of Isaiah. I would first read the Old Testament chapters and then read from several commentaries. One day I read Isaiah 49:15 which says, "Can a woman forget her sucking child, that she should not have compassion on the son of her womb? yea, they may forget, yet will I not forget thee." Much of Isaiah had been a mystery to me, but as I read that verse my heart jumped and tears came to my eyes. I didn't need the commentators to realize the deep significance and expression of love in that verse.

But as I read what the commentaries had to say I was surprised at how they had missed the point. Each one said something about how God has blessed women with a strong emotional bond of love for their children and how the Lord's love is even stronger than that. But a mother's love may not have been the real point of this verse. Mother's love is not a universal thing. Some mothers don't have any love. Hardly a week goes by that you don't read an account of a mother beating or abandoning her child; even innocent little newborns are left in trash cans to die! Isaiah's verse doesn't say much if it only means that the Lord has more love for us than that.

To my mind the key to the meaning of the verse is the word *sucking* or nursing child. "Can a woman forget her sucking child?" A woman who has nursed a baby knows that when feeding time comes, even if the child still sleeps, the mother remembers the child. An increasing milk supply is painful. It is an internal alarm that *will not* allow the woman to forget that she has a child to feed. Regardless of whether she wants to or not, there is no way she can forget because of the pain. Yet, the Lord says, she may overlook the pain, but his remembrance of us will be even more compelling. Seen in that light, the promise, "Behold, I have graven thee upon the palms of my hands; thy walls are continually before me" (Isaiah 49:16) becomes much more significant.

Another example is found in Paul's words: "What? know ye not that your body is the temple of the Holy Ghost which is in you, which ye have of God, and ye are not your own? For ye are bought with a price: therefore glorify God in your body, and in your spirit, which are God's." (1 Corinthians 6:19–20.) A woman who out of love has given birth to or raised a child knows what it means to suffer in order to give another life, and the emotional bond thus created. As a woman I *know* that we are not our own. We are connected through bonds of pain and suffering especially to our mothers but also to our fathers; and if that be the case, how much greater the connection to Jesus Christ, who suffered for our sins? We are literally his. We owe our lives to him. He bought us with his blood and with his flesh. The argument that "It is my life, I'll do what I want to do," thus loses all credibility!

As men and women we share unique life experiences that we should ponder and learn from. For example, as a woman shares with her husband the feelings and emotions inherent in taking someone else's name upon her in marriage, as she is able to articulate the emotionally significant experiences associated with changing her name, her identifying title, both will understand more of what it means to take the Savior's name upon us and what we need to do to accomplish this important step.

There are many places in the scriptures that speak not only to a woman's intellectual understanding but also to her experience, just as there are many scriptures that speak to a man's experience and understanding. As a husband and wife study together, both contributing to the discussion, both bringing their own experience to the scriptures, they will grow not only spiritually but also in unity. The sharing of such feelings is one of the greatest bonding experiences there is. It strengthens the couple's love and creates a deeper, more meaningful level of intimacy, a level that is necessary in order for the Holy Spirit of Promise to seal the marriage for eternity.

Emphasis has been made in the Church that helps us understand the role played by a worthy priesthood office holder. As we further explore those concepts and then learn more about the help meet, woman, we will all be enriched. As more and more women follow President Kimball's admonition to become scholars of the scriptures, not only the women will be enlightened but so will the men and the children. We will receive new and meaningful insights that will help us live the gospel of Jesus Christ more completely.

After we have learned and shared, we then need to teach our children what we have learned. We need to teach them the gospel of Jesus Christ. We need to teach our young men and our young women nurturing and relationship skills. We need to teach them the significance of priesthood and help meet, fatherhood and motherhood, handmaiden and servant to the Lord. Before they marry we need to help them understand what the Lord intended marriage to be, so that they can better choose a marriage partner and go on to achieve their full potential.

Serve One Another
and the Lord

Adam and Eve served each other and the Lord.

A friend told me of a couple she knew who had struggled with their marriage relationship. The wife said that one day her husband announced that he was going away for the weekend, and as he packed his bag she realized that she didn't care if he never came back. This awareness alarmed her so much that when he did return she insisted that the two of them sit down for a long discussion about what had happened to their relationship and what they should do.

Their solution was most interesting. Instead of divorcing, instead of following only the precepts of men and working to increase their communication skills or have more positive attitudes, this couple decided that they needed to more fully live the gospel. These were active Church members who had held key positions in their ward, but they felt that they had been active in more of a social way than in a spiritual way. They decided to study the scriptures together and as a family and to try to implement what they learned while studying. They decided to hold regular family home evenings. They decided to honestly give all that they could to their Church callings and to support and help each other in those callings. The only goal they set that one would think was directly related to the marriage was a goal to spend more time together.

Three years later everyone who knew them had seen a dramatic change in their lives. They were very different people. When the husband was made an elders quorum president, his wife said that she could see the mantle of the calling as it came to him and that she knew he was worthy of the call. Then she remarked, "I don't know how I could ever live without that man."

The righteous union of man and woman for time and eternity begins at an altar. As a couple kneel across from one another the altar is between them. This is significant. The altar is a symbol of sacrifice; Old Testament sacrifices were made at and on altars. Sacrifice is necessary to make the connection between the man and the woman, the connection that binds them into a celestial unit. There must be sacrifice! Wives must sacrifice for husbands and husbands must sacrifice for wives; but most important, both must sacrifice for the Lord. In this way each achieves his or her full potential and accomplishes his or her duties and missions in life. The sacrifice cannot be one-sided if it is to achieve this. It cannot be half-hearted. It cannot be motivated by selfish or impure desires.

This sacrifice must start by understanding the spouse's role and the importance of that role in the marriage. A woman must understand the importance of her husband's exercising his priesthood authority—not only for her own but also for her husband's salvation; and the man must understand the importance of the giving of life and fulfilling the duties of help meet—not only for his own but also for his wife's salvation.

If either men or women had been given both the stewardships of government and creation, the other would be drones in society. They would not be needed and would have no specific way to contribute, to serve, and to sacrifice in order to gain salvation. We each need to *do* something in order to inherit eternal life. It is important that each of us perform our assigned labors in order to maintain the balance and to work out our own salvation. A woman who takes over her husband's role and does not allow him to preside dams his progression. A man who dictates to his wife, not allowing her to contribute her talents and abilities, dams her progression. Letting one another serve and sacrifice and thus grow is as important as serving and sacrificing oneself.

In the Old Testament there is a powerful story that teaches us what happens to people when they don't let others perform their God-given assignments. Saul was chosen by the Lord to be king because he was "a choice young man, and a goodly: and there was not among the children of Israel a goodlier person than he" (1 Samuel 9:2). In the beginning of his reign he lived by the Spirit, he followed the prophet Samuel, and he gave God credit for all he did. But it seems that after a few battles and the taste of victory and glory, he began to decline spiritually.

Before a battle with the Philistines, the prophet Samuel had instructed Saul to wait for him in Gilgal seven days until he could come to make a sacrificial offering. But as Saul waited he grew impatient. His armies, fearing the Philistines, who were gathering for battle, began to scatter. Worried and faithless Saul performed the ordinance himself. Just as he finished, Samuel arrived and asked, "What hast thou done?"

Saul told Samuel that the gathering Philistines were scaring away his armies, and then he justified himself as follows: "Therefore said I, The Philistines will come down now upon me to Gilgal, and I have not made supplication unto the Lord: I forced myself therefore, and offered a burnt offering".

Saul was king, but he had no priesthood authority to perform the ordinance of sacrifice and was not directed by the Spirit; therefore he had sinned. As a consequence he was told, "thy kingdom shall not continue . . . because thou hast not kept that which the Lord commanded thee." (1 Samuel 13:11–14.) Because Saul assumed the duties of Samuel's stewardship, he lost his own stewardship: his kingdom.

We should also recognize that in the struggle that too often occurs over roles in a marriage or a culture, the basic problem always comes back to control and power. One or both want the power to control the other. But such control is against everything the gospel stands for. During our first estate each of us fought against the idea of another person controlling us. This realization should help us to pull back if we find ourselves seeking to control another or to exercise unrighteous dominion, and to think about whom we are emulating.

Pray and Obey

Adam and Eve called upon the Lord and did what he told them to do.

Much of the counsel we hear from our modern prophet is aimed at strengthening the family unit—the most important unit of both mortality and immortality. The counsel he gives must be heeded if we want to become gods. But Satan is throwing his most vicious attacks at destroying marriages as God intended them to be.

This isn't a problem that is going to go away, but it is one we must actively fight. The positions of father and mother, husband and wife have been greatly demeaned in our culture. Instead of placing good relationships as one of our highest values, we have begun more highly to value material acquisition, recreation, and self-fulfillment. If we are going to save marriages, save families, we need to recognize the importance of priesthood office and help meet, of husband and wife, of motherhood and fatherhood. We need to call upon the Lord and ask how best to fulfill these sacred stewardships.

As married couples we need to evaluate our lives to see how much we do because of tradition and the precepts of men and how much we do because it fits the blueprint or because it is God's will. Elder George Q. Cannon said: "Traditions . . . that are so difficult for us to overcome . . . interfere so seriously with the progress of the people in the things of God. . . . It is only when the Spirit of God rests upon us . . . that we can understand and comprehend the power of tradition over our minds and conduct." (*Journal of Discourses* 13:368–69.) One by one we need to cast the traditions of men out of our lives and replace them with the precepts of God. In this way great peace and a harmony that vibrates into the hearts of the entire family are brought into a marriage.

One of the great keys to this power and strength is found in the acknowledgment that all of our effort must be spent on *being* the right marriage partner. So much time and effort is wasted in trying to change a spouse. We too often fail to realize that the only person who can change another is the Holy Ghost. That is his steward-ship. When we try to change others we are infringing upon the stewardship of the Holy Spirit. We can influence, we can love, we can provide example and an environment where the Spirit can dwell, but we cannot change anyone else.

When we study and learn all that we can in order to be the best spouse possible, we quit worrying about what the other person does or does not do and worry instead about the condition of our own heart. Are our motives pure? Are we full of faith and hope and charity? Are we giving to the relationship all that we can? Are we helping create an atmosphere in which the Spirit can dwell? Are we seeking and doing the Lord's will? Are we selflessly considering the needs of our spouse?

Some people desire the Eden relationship knowing full well that their partner does not. They desire to change, to do the things they need to do, but know the partner doesn't. What of these people? The fact that we cannot change others becomes even more important in these cases. Trying to change such a person only makes things worse. Our only hope is to call upon the Lord and to do what he tells us to do, all the while being the best spouse we can be.

A friend of mine who had been a bishop shared an interesting story with me. A woman came to him asking what to do about her inactive husband. She wanted the kind of marriage we have been talking about; she wanted her children to be raised in the Church. Her husband had let her take their two sons to church while they were small, but now that the boys were older he wanted them to go hunting and fishing with him on Sundays.

After this woman had described the fighting and contention that was tearing apart her life, the bishop asked, "What does the Spirit tell you to do?"

She was startled. "Of course the Spirit would tell me to take my boys to church!" she said.

"Have you prayed and received that answer?"

"Well, no."

"Then you had better pray about it."

A week later the woman returned. She was very quiet, but at peace. "I can't believe the answer I have received," she said, "but I know it is of the Spirit. The answer is that not only should I let the boys go with Bill, but I should go too."

For the next two years this woman patiently and without complaint packed and traveled and camped and fished on the Sabbath even though she longed to be in church. At the end of two long years, and without any forewarning, her husband suddenly announced: "I don't like what is happening to you and the boys. You are changing. I have decided that you and the boys should go back to church, and I want to come with you."

This kind of example is not far-fetched. The problem is that too many of us read such a story and then do a similar thing only to find it doesn't work for us. Then we doubt. But the reason it worked for this woman is because the Spirit told her to do it. That is the secret. We must live close to the Lord and do what the Spirit tells *us* to do, not what the Spirit directed a neighbor to do.

President Marion G. Romney gave some very timely advice when he said, "There would be no dissensions or divorces in our homes, if we would there subject ourselves to the guidance of the Holy Spirit" (*Relief Society Magazine,* October 1955, p. 648).

No matter what state our relationships are in before we begin to build or to rebuild them, prayer and the guidance of the Spirit coupled with unselfish love are the most powerful tools we have to use. As a matter of fact an Eden relationship can *only* be built as directed by the Spirit, because the exact procedure, the exact building materials, the number of rooms, the exact type of house to be built will be different for every couple.

As we concentrate on our own behavior, as we pray for guidance, as we live the commandments, we invite the Spirit into our relationships. We allow the Spirit to work in our hearts to recreate us in the image of Christ. It is by this process that we experience joy, love, and peace in a world that knows so little of these things.

Our Father in Heaven and our Savior want us to be conformed to their likeness. As we turn to them for help in our marriages they will guide us to the faith, hope, and charity that we need, as well as to the specific things we must do. As we ask and seek they will help us to find resources, knowledge, and strength that we never imagined possible. We will be able to make our marriage richer, happier, and more celestial, and we will be able to fulfill our own destiny and callings—to do all that we have been sent to earth to do.

From Eternity to Eternity

The potential for extraordinary marriage relationships is in the gospel of Jesus Christ. The rewards for seeking the potential are eternally significant. The foundation and purpose of the gospel are found in our maleness and femaleness, and as we come to understand these things better we will reach new heights of spiritual and marital fulfillment. We will begin to understand what President Brigham Young meant when he said:

> The whole subject of the marriage relation is not in my reach, nor in any other man's reach on this earth. It is without beginning of days or end of years; it is a hard matter to reach. We can tell some things with regard to it; it lays the foundation for worlds, for angels, and for the Gods; for intelligent beings to be crowned with glory, immortality, and eternal lives. In fact, it is the thread which runs from the beginning to the end of the holy Gospel of salvation — of the Gospel of the Son of God; it is from eternity to eternity. (*Journal of Discourses* 2:90.)

As we catch the vision of why we are male and female, as we learn more about eternal marriage, we draw a marvelous blueprint. Once we have the blueprint, not only will we know what we are building and why, but also the Spirit will guide us as to how we should build it. Then, and only then, will our earthly homes be the beginning of our celestial life.

Index

Chastity that includes total fidelity of thoughts bonds the husband and wife in "onement." It invites God into the relationship. It gives the couple power and strength to become one with God. President Joseph F. Smith said, "There appears to be a something beyond and above the reasons apparent to the human mind why chastity brings strength and power to the peoples of the earth, but it is so" (*Gospel Doctrine* [Salt Lake City: Deseret Book Company, 1971], p. 274).

Elder John A. Widtsoe said, "Chastity is the strongest bulwark against the many temptations of life" ("Woman's Greatest Career," *Improvement Era,* October 1940, p. 637).

Fidelity to one's spouse, loyalty, allegiance, devotion, attachment in thoughts, words, and deeds not only make for a happy marriage during earth life but also are essential for the marriage to be sealed by the Holy Spirit of Promise.

Chastity: Using Procreative Power in Marriage

Satan's counterfeit for chastity is celibacy. Celibacy within marriage, unless that is commanded by God in a particular instance, is wrong. Within the marriage covenant sexual union is important for giving spirits earthly bodies, for bonding the man and the woman, and for the growth and development of the couple.

While watching a recently born colt struggle on new, spindly legs, I was suddenly struck with the thought that here was one of God's creatures—a mammal like man—that within hours of birth could walk and within weeks would be independent of the mare who had given it life. My mind jumped to others of the animal kingdom who are hatched after parents have physically left. These animals are on their own from the first seconds of life. Why, then, did God create human children to be dependent upon parents for years? Why aren't humans able to walk away from their own nativity? If God made other animals so independent of parents, couldn't he have created man to be independent also?

As I pondered the flood of questions, it occurred to me that perhaps God created human babies to be dependent not so much for the baby's sake as for the parents' sake. If babies were born, walked, talked, and soon left, what growth would parents have?

Relationships, and "onement," 92–93
Relief Society, organizing of, 70
Repentance, alternative to divorce, 106
  continuance in, 73
Responsibilities, uniting power of, 25
Responsibility, burden of presiding man, 27
Revelation, to women, 30
Righteousness, crown of, 75
Roles, based on righteousness, 45
  intertwined and interdependent, 67
Ruach, meaning of, 78

Sacrifice, binds marriage, 119
  essential for spiritual growth, 77
  labeled as stupid by world, 84
  of personal desire if worthy of priest-
    hood, 61
Salome, 39
Salvation, assisted by faithful endurance, 19
  individual and family effort, 114
  marriage partner's contribution, 33
  of priesthood holder dependent on
    service, 65
Samaritan woman, 40
Samson, mother of, 30
Samuel, 27
Sarah, 79
Satan, 13
  demeans motherhood, 84
  enmity to mankind, 15
  fosters misunderstanding of eternal
    principles, 3–4
  goal is discord, 93
  tries to undermine chastity, 106–7
  wanted power and control, 45
  worldly philosophies of, 4
Saul, 120
Saviors, priesthood bearers, 53
Scripture study, husband and wife
  together, 117
Scriptures, no validation for male
  superiority, 25
  show balance of "he" and "she," 24
  show establishment of male-female
    relationship, 5–6
  to be expounded by women, 74
Selfishness, enemy to righteousness, 60
  in marriage, 91
Separation, Satan's attempts on Adam and
  Eve, 12–13
Service, 59
  responsibility of call to preside, 27
  road to godhood, 55
Shiprah, 71
Smith, Emma, God's instructions to, 72
  revelation applicable to all women, 72

Snow, Eliza R., organization of women's
  group, 70
Sorrow, consequences of Fall, 16
Spiritual gifts, 23
  equal access by men and women, 4–5, 32
Spouse, being the best one can be, 122
  encouragement of, 95
Stereotypes, righteous roles preferable to, 48
Steward, term applied to priesthood bearer, 59
Stewards, of life, 78
  over gospel ordinances, 59
Stewardships, equivalency in, 76
  men's and women's overlap, 70
  of both husband and wife are in home, 70
  of government and creation, 119–20
  prayer on how to fulfill, 121
  priesthood and fatherhood, 64
  symbolically represented in scriptures, 77
Submission, must be freely given, 25
  of body to spirit, 25
  of Jesus to Father, 43
  required of all, 25
Sun, referred to as "he," 23
Symbolism, of rib, 12
  principles learned from, 26
Synergism, creates celestial unit, 101
  in Eden relationship, 89

Traditions, can have power over minds, 121
  dictate husband-wife relationships, 99–100
  feelings of male superiority established
    by, 25
  not always correct, 4
  preventing "onement," 26
Tree of knowledge, 8
Tree of life, 8

Understanding, foundation of marriage, 5
Unity, 34

Vows, by Old Testament women, 26–27

Whitmer, Mary Musselman, shown golden
  plates by messenger, 68
Wife, success as, 84
  supportive of husband in callings, 75
  to be comfort to husband, 73
  to follow husband in righteousness, 62, 94
  to judge how husband presides, 62